The Trout at the Walnut Tree

NOTES FROM A FLY-FISHING JOURNAL

by Richard Tate

Published by

krause
publications
700 East State St.   Iola WI 54990
715-445-2214

Library of Congress Catalog Number: 91-61305
ISBN: 0-87341-167-6
Printed in the United States of America

CONTENTS

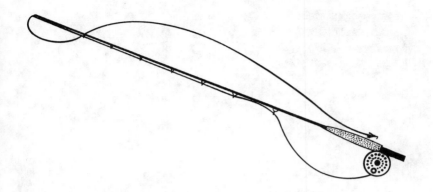

INTRODUCTION

The late 1960s and early 1970s were a turbulent time in America. While American youth were bravely fighting and dying in steamy Southeast Asian jungles, equally courageous Americans such as Joan Baez were striving heroically to end the awful slaughter.

Instead of worrying about the war, I was developing an interest in fly-fishing for trout. This interest developed gradually, and as time passed, this interest turned into passion.

As this passion progressed, I discovered the literature about fly-fishing. My early bible was Ray Bergman's classic, *Trout,* and I tried to apply Bergman's teachings to my own fishing. Later, my development was influenced by other writers, most notably Vincent Marinaro, Ernest Schweibert, and Leonard Wright. Marinaro's *A Modern Dry Fly Code* helped me to analyze the way mayfly hatches develop and how different stages of a hatch influence trout feeding behavior. The information about terrestrials was helpful to me, too. Schweibert's *Matching the Hatch* was the reference I used to try to identify hatches on the waters I fished and, in my opinion, still ranks as one of the two best entomological texts for fly-fishermen, the other being Caucci and Nastasia's *Hatches.* Leonard Wright's *Fishing the Dry Fly as a Living Insect* aided me in my quest to find flies that were effective when there was no visible feeding activity.

5

One of fly-fishing's lovely rewards is a trout.

I did not confine my reading to books of instruction: I found quite a few that dealt with the joys of trout, as Arnold Gingrich so aptly called non-instructive writings. William Schaldach's lovely books, Charles Fox's *This Wonderful World of Trout,* Schweibert's *Remembrances of Rivers Past,* and Haig-Brown's *A River Never Sleeps* were among the best. But my personal favorite was Robert Traver's wonderful *Trout Madness,* in which Traver (Judge John Voelker) writes vividly about many of his fishing adventures. His later *Trout Magic* is a fine companion piece. The two Traver books and Norman Maclean's marvelous *A River Runs Through It* are the most frequently read books in my fishing library.

My regular fishing partners of those days, Bruce Houck and Dan Deters, and I often discussed the books we'd read and how we sometimes disagreed with what an author had written. "When I write my book," one of us often laughed, "this is what I would say."

To me that was pretty serious: I really was developing a desire to write a book. And now I've finally done it.

Ahead of you there are chapters that show how I evolved into a trout fly- fisherman, chapters that are intended to be instructive, and chapters that are included strictly to entertain. You will discover that I fish trout streams that are similar to ones that many flyrodders fish, at least here in the East where coldwater streams have been degraded and abused for a couple of centuries. That many possess the ability to harbor trout at all is a tribute to their resiliency in the face of the destruction that man calls progress. I have learned to appreciate the values of modest-sized trout on modest-sized, public-access trout waters where a 15-inch brown is a dandy, especially if it is a streambred fish.

As you read *The Trout at the Walnut Tree,* I hope you will share my enthusiasm for the pursuit of trout with flies — and that you will overlook my often too-serious approach: I know that I don't take time to "smell the roses" along trout steams often enough. Most of all, I hope that *The Trout at the Walnut Tree* strikes a responsive chord for you as a fellow fly-fisherman.

Richard Tate, Williamsburg, PA

The author works his way upstream on a small creek, enthusiastically pursuing his reward — a trout.

Chapter 1

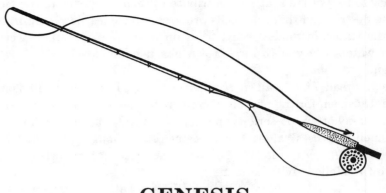

GENESIS,
Part I

When I was 18 years old, I decided to become a trout fisherman. Sure, I had fished for trout previously, but I'd never been very serious about it. Most of my spare time had previously been occupied by high school sports, especially basketball, and I had never really had the time or the desire to learn to fish for trout. From my previous experiences, I considered trout fishing to be an arcane activity, but I figured that if I worked as hard at learning to fish as I had at learning to play basketball, eventually I'd solve the mysteries of trout fishing.

There weren't many enthusiastic trout fishermen in my hometown in 1968, and of the ones I knew, few were willing to divulge any of their secrets. Most of these fellows fished with live bait, mostly with striped minnows, from what I could gather.

I was in my first year of college at the time, and I was able to devote only so much time to my fishing. After all, I did have to study, and a good bit of the rest of my time was devoted to the rituals that teenage boys seem to have to undergo. As one of my friends said years later about our escapades, we certainly tried to self-destruct in those days. It was a pretty accurate assessment.

I was not too particular about how I caught trout. I really thought that live minnow fishing was the best route to take, and I equipped myself with a stout flyrod and automatic reel as I set out after the trout on small local creeks. I never caught a trout on a minnow. I tried mornings and evenings; clear water and muddied water; large minnows and small ones; but nothing ever worked. I eventually turned to my opening day stand-by: earthworms. Using these in high, cloudy water, I began to catch an occasional trout, some nice ones by local standards, too. In one of my old scrapbooks, I have a snapshot of myself proudly holding a brace of 15-inch browns, the best fish I managed to take that year, and I was all smiles. If the truth be told, a 15-inch brown still brings me a satisfied smile on most of the creeks I fish.

The worm fishing, however, did not result in consistently successful outings. I really didn't catch very many trout for the number of hours I was astream. I kept notes about my fishing trips, and they reveal that I probably averaged only about one trout for every four or five hours of fishing, and that isn't very good by anyone's standards. I was persistent, though.

I suppose the first real breakthrough came on May 13 of that year. Bruce Houck, my sister's husband, who was then her boyfriend, and I had decided to try an evening of fishing. I was toting my trusty night crawlers; Bruce, who knew a little about fly-fishing, was going to use flies. He had a Royal Coachman, as I recall.

Bruce went upstream; I began to fish downstream where I ran into Ralph Haney, one of the few real fly-fishermen in town. He and his son, Randy, were waiting for a hatch of flies to activate the trout, and

A respectable brown trout can be caught using a variety of methods, but fly-fishing is one of the best.

9

as they waited, I pestered Ralph into showing me how to flycast. He did, and soon he was into a trout. My notes reveal that I was skunked that evening, but Ralph and Randy both caught several fine trout. One of Randy's was a very large brown trout.

After this demonstration on the effectiveness of fly-fishing, I decided I was going to try it. My dad had a half-dozen flies squirreled away, and he knew enough to tell me to buy a tapered leader and some tippet material if I was going to try to fly-fish. When I bought these, I also bought myself a half-dozen flies to use on the little creeks I was going to fish.

It was five days later that I caught my first trout on a fly. The creeks had been muddied by rains, but by the eighteenth, they had cleared enough for me to try my flies. The locals called the flies that were hatching *Beaverkills,* and the egg layers, which sported colorful orange egg sacs, were dubbed *Yellow Beaverkills* or *Female Beaverkills.* It was years later that I finally realized that these were heavy hatches and spinner falls of what most knowledgeable fly-fishermen refer to as Sulphurs: *Ephemerella rotunda, invaria,* and *dorothea.* However, it didn't much matter what you called them, especially if you were an 18-year-old neophyte.

I tied on a size 14 Female Beaverkill dry fly I had "borrowed" from Dad. It accounted for two ten-inch trout that evening, and I was hooked forever on dry-fly fishing for trout.

I was no purist, though, and every time it rained that summer, I tried to rise at daybreak and be astream. It was a recognized "fact" around town that trout fed best in the early morning, especially after rains. As a newcomer to trout fishing, I was in no position to contradict this sage, sound maxim. In addition, it permitted me to fish for a couple of hours before I went off to work at my summer job as lifeguard at a small state park. Actually, lifeguarding was more of a position than a job, and it was a sad day a couple summers later when I had to give up watching the sights at the beach to take a summer job at a paper mill. But the mill job paid a lot better than lifeguarding did, and extra money was a rare commodity for me during my college days.

Those hours of bait fishing in the early hours resulted in some trout, but I often philosophized about how nice it was just to be out. Any serious angler will tell you that's a bunch of baloney. Time passes pretty slowly when you're not catching anything, and no matter how many deer, scarlet tanagers or rabbits you run into while you're fishing, they in no way can ever measure up to that satisfying tug that a trout provides at the end of your line.

By August, I'd given up the early morning outings and was devoting my fishing time to evening affairs using flies. I never caught more than six trout during any excursion that year, but I usually caught at least one or two fish while fly-fishing. I knew that I could become a consistently successful trout fisherman if I perfected my fly-fishing skills; I would be able to catch far more trout on flies than I could on live bait. However, at 35 or 40 cents per fly, I knew that I was going to run out of money learning to fly-fish because I lost one or more flies each time I was on the creek.

By Labor Day, I had caught 55 trout, more than 30 of which had been taken on flies, but because I was out of flies and the money to buy more, I decided to end the season (Labor Day was then Pennsylvania's closing day) using live bait: crickets and grasshoppers. My comment about the season's last day was this: ". . . and, as usual with live bait, I got skunked."

"Ralph Haney did a good job of setting me up," the author said of his fly tying equipment, which is expensive. The author received his fly tying equipment from his mother and father for Christmas one year, "probably the best Christmas gift I ever received," he said.

I knew darned well that fly-fishing was the best way to catch trout, but how could I afford it? Ralph Haney and Christmas came to my rescue. Ralph was one of the few guys around who tied his own flies, and he told me that if I bought the equipment to tie flies, he would show me how. He gave me a Herter's catalog and showed me what to order. I filled out an order form, and Dad and Mom bought me all the items Ralph had told me I'd need to get started. "That is all you're getting for Christmas," Mom told me. It was plenty, probably the best Christmas gift I ever received. I have, however, successfully

11

avoided tying commercially: I believe that trying to sell flies would ruin fly tying for me.

The tools I bought from Herter's were "A-Number 1" stuff. I still have all those old Herter's tools I bought, and except for the vise and bobbin, I still use them. I would still use the bobbin, too, but today's spools of tying thread do not work in it, and I've had to settle for a more modern, less satisfactory clip bobbin. No modern manufacturer has ever come up with a whip finisher to match my old Herter's "trout size" model. I once owned two Herter's trout size whip finishers, but I foolishly traded one away in return for information about tying and using braided Stonefly nymphs. Today, I'd prefer to have that old Herter's tool, and I'd surely panic if I ever lost the one I have remaining.

Ralph shared good, solid information with me as I began to tie. After he had showed me the basics of tying, he told me the flies I'd need: the Female Beaverkill, a tan fly he called a Cahill, a Light Cahill, a Gray-Hackle Peacock, and an Adams, all tied dry. That's not a very long list, but four of these flies still figure prominently in my fishing. I sometimes use the Adams to fish the water when no fish are rising; I use a Cream Variant and its variations (much like Ralph's Light Cahill) to match hatches of cream mayflies; I use a Gray-Hackle Peacock wet fly for some underwater prospecting; and I use the tan fly to imitate the Sulphurs on my favorite trout waters. I finally quit tying the Female Beaverkill: It never accounted for many large fish for me, and when I discovered that the female Sulphurs dropped their eggs before they died and fell to the stream, I realized why the Female Beaverkill wasn't a real deadly fly. It matched flies in the air, not ones that were on the water. Ralph, however, swore by the flies with the egg sacs, and I saw him catch a good many trout on them when I was learning to fly-fish. They just never worked very well for me.

I tied flies assiduously all that winter, and when the next season arrived, I had a box full of what I thought were real trout flies. I'm afraid what I used in those days would be throw-aways today, but they caught trout about as well as my casting ability would allow. Most of these flies were tied on size 14 and 16 hooks, as my flies are today. These Herter's hooks were better than any I've acquired since, and I still have a couple hundred Herter's Number 5029T dry fly hooks that I use to tie my Sulphur spinners. Modern manufacturers, even the fanatical Japanese, haven't equalled this hook, in my opinion.

The 1969 season was a real trial-and-error learning experience. Though I fished an occasional nightcrawler, of the 60-odd days I spent astream, more than 50 were spent fly-fishing. I was rapidly becoming a fly-fishing purist, and by the following season, I had almost sworn off bait fishing for good, except on native brook trout streams where I continued to drown worms until I graduated from college.

Brook trout streams, I now realize, are pretty special here in Pennsylvania. These wild, often remote brooks flow clear and cold and offer the best early season fishing for trout. When the water is high in the spring, these freestone brooks are at their best, unlike larger waters which fish better as the water levels drop. Over the years, I have found that a tandem of wet flies, one always being a Royal Coachman, will take trout regularly on these gorgeous mountain brooks. Acid rain is adversely affecting these fragile natural resources, though I hope that legislation will soon be enacted that will help to preserve them for future generations.

At any rate, 1969 provided a great deal of action. By the end of the season, I had caught 236 trout, a total that I thought was pretty remarkable. My trusty flies took trout up to 14 inches, which is a respectable fish in my bailiwick. In those days, I thought that 14-inch trout were veritable monsters. My fly box took a terrible beating, though. Of the hundreds of flies that crowded its compartments at the beginning of the season, only a few remained on closing day. I left many in trees and bushes; a large number snapped off my leader as I "cracked the whip" when casting; and many more were attached to the mouths of trout that I lost on the strike.

The author concentrates on a trout.

The timing of my casting left much to be desired. I suppose a casting instructor at a fly-fishing school could have cured my problems quickly, but I would not trade my early experiences and frustrations for the quick-fixes a school could have provided. My trial-and-error initiation into the world of fly-fishing was an education in itself.

Probably the most important thing I was learning was where to fish. I was discovering areas of the local streams that boasted fine populations of trout, while other areas looking as if they ought to be productive, were nearly barren of fish. Over the past 20 years, I have stashed away a lot of this information, and it has helped me to be more consistently successful than I was during the late 1960s.

Reading the water was another part of this education. As the season rushed by, I began to realize that trout were not spread evenly throughout a stream, even in its productive sections. I discovered that they favored small pockets of shaded water in meadow areas, and places my dad called "green water," deeper pockets and pools in rapid-moving water; these were good trout lairs. Of course, the deep, mysterious holes surrendered a few trout as darkness set in, and today I often try to end a fishing day on a large pool. I have found that the larger trout on my favorite waters often come out to feed about this time.

To the best of my recollection, 1969 was the year the state fish commission first opened trout streams to fishing after Labor Day. Only a few streams were left open that year, but one of them was one of my favorites, and I managed a few autumn fishing trips. By Labor Day, I was feeling pretty smug about how great a fly-fisherman I had become, but when I saw the large numbers of trout that seemed to appear from nowhere that fall, I realized that I caught only a small percentage of the trout that were available to be caught. I also realized that 14-inch trout, while respectable, were not the creek's lunkers.

In mid-October I spotted a few fish of 18 to 20 inches on their spawning beds, and I knew that there were a few real battlewagons that I was going to lust after for many years. Of the entire trout season, I think early autumn, the time from Sept. 10 to Oct. 20, is usually the nicest to be astream. The streamside colors are gorgeous, the creeks are generally clear and cold, and the trout are feeding aggressively as they prepare for spawning and the rigors of winter. The trout highlight of the 1969 season was the autumn day that I caught two 14-inch browns and a 12-inch brown in about 45 minutes of fishing. This extended season limit of three trout was the nicest trio of fish I had ever brought home at one time, and I was pretty proud of myself that afternoon.

A typical small stream in central Pennsylvania can yield good amounts of trout, especially if the stream is not overfished.

The next two seasons progressed much as the '69 season had. I found that my local streams did not fish very well until about mid-May, but they fished well all summer long once they began to be productive. These creeks received plantings of hatchery fish in those years, and I suppose this influx of competitors disrupted the patterns of the streams' wild trout so badly that the wild fish didn't return to their normal patterns until May. However, even today, I do not do well on these streams until early- to mid-May; so perhaps my early observations weren't so off-base after all.

I continued to learn various stream sections that were productive, and my casting improved greatly. I lost fewer and fewer flies to the wind as my timing improved. I landed more of the larger trout — 12 inches and over — that I hooked, and I became increasingly confident in my abilities. When I read an article in a national magazine about a guy who had caught 300 trout in a season, I felt really good. If he was an expert, then I was rapidly becoming pretty proficient, too, or so I thought.

I spent increasing amounts of time on trout streams, while at the same time trying to keep my grades up in school and trying to maintain a semblance of a normal social life. Perhaps the best move I made during those years was transferring from the Penn State system to Lock Haven State College, now Lock Haven University. Besides receiving a superior education at Lock Haven, I discovered some fine trout streams nearby, streams that I still visit. The freestone trout streams of north-central Pennsylvania are among the loveliest anywhere, and when I did a part of my practice teaching in Renovo, I fished some dandy streams that seemed like trout Heaven to me.

During those years, I also discovered one of the perils of fly-fishing. Fishing was occupying ever increasing amounts of my time, and that's not really too healthy in a love relationship. I was steadily dating a lovely woman in those final years of college, and we shared some good times. However, as time passed, our dates began to revolve more and more around my fishing schedule. I also dragged her along on many of my excursions, expecting her to read or to pick flowers as I fished. She probably knew as much about the local trout streams as I did. One evening she found a pod of rising trout for me, of which I kept five that I caught. I traded these for a bag of morels her father had found that day. My mother loved morels, and she thought I had made a great deal.

Another evening, when I was preparing to knock a trout on the head to kill it, my girlfriend said, "Oh, Richard, let it go. It is too pretty to kill."

I had been releasing trout under 10 inches, but when I looked at the wild trout, I had to agree with her: It was indeed too lovely to kill, and from that day on, I have become increasingly a catch-and-release trout fisherman.

Finally, though, the woman had enough, and when she broke up with me, she cited my preoccupation with fly-fishing as one of the major reasons. I was devastated: My heart was broken, and my ego was shattered. It's kind of a joke in fly-fishing literature that fly-fishing contributes to lost jobs and broken marriages. Though I was not married at the time, I am living proof that fly-fishing does contribute to destroyed love relationships, and it is really no joke.

I once heard a doctor say that fly-fishing isn't a hobby: It's a way of life. Fly-fishermen build their lives around their fishing and their fly tying, and other aspects of their lives must be satellites to their angling. At this stage of my life, I suppose the doctor was right. Everything I did revolved around my fly-fishing, so much, in fact, that my own mother often told me that I was eccentric. She was doubtlessly correct.

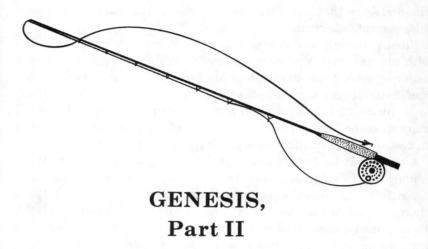

Chapter 2

GENESIS,
Part II

The three seasons after my graduation from college in 1971 witnessed the most rapid improvements ever in my development as a fly-fisherman. My casting improved, my recognition of different kinds of flies progressed, and my ability to catch trout improved dramatically.

By the conclusion of the 1971 season, I thought I was a pretty hotshot trout fisherman. For three consecutive years I had caught 200 or more trout, and I was pretty impressed with my performances. In addition, the flies I tied had improved to the point that other people sometimes asked me to sell them some. It was a temptation that I resisted. Fly tying is a nice hobby, but its eye-straining, meticulous nature makes it a frustrating job.

Bruce's fishing development was paralleling mine, though up to our graduation from college, he used store-bought flies. Upon his graduation, Anne, my sister, presented him with the tools and materials needed to tie flies. I'm surprised that Bruce's fly tying didn't cause them to have marital problems during their first year: That winter, not long after their marriage on Oct. 23, he and I began to spend a lot of late nights tying flies in the basement of my parents' home. Of course, Bruce and Anne were only there on weekends: Bruce had gotten a teaching job 50 miles away, and they lived in a small apartment there while Anne completed her college education.

Some of the flies we created during those late-night tying sessions

It takes concentration to whip up a good fly. Dan Deters, shown at work on the vise, creates a mayfly to work a little magic.

might best be forgotten, if they hadn't worked so surprisingly well on the trout.

It was about this time that we became friends with a pair of men with whom we fished a great deal over the years. I became acquainted with Dan Deters while playing volleyball, and one evening after a three-game match, he asked me about fly-fishing. I was eager to share some stories, which finally led him to ask me if I'd help him learn to tie flies.

"Sure," I told him, "I'll be glad to. You're already a catch-and-release fisherman, and I think you'd like fly-fishing."

I gave Dan a couple lessons, he got some pointers from another fellow, and he became a regular fishing partner. In fact, he joined Bruce and me on so many of our trips that I'm sure his patient wife, Sue, sometimes saw less of him than we did. That Dan has become a gentleman angler over the years and is a credit to the sport is due in large part to Sue's understanding. He'll tell you that.

The other man we got to know was Henry Malone of Milesburg. Henry was in his last year of teaching during Bruce's rookie year as a faculty member at Bald Eagle Area High School, and Henry took Bruce under his wing that year. When Henry discovered Bruce's budding interest as a fly-fisherman, their friendship became even more solid. Henry showed Bruce some good places to fish in north-central Pennsylvania, and Dan and I tagged along on many of the trips to these streams. Henry also shared some fly patterns with us that have become mainstays in our fly boxes. Bruce, Dan, and I owe a great deal to Henry Malone, one of the finest gentlemen I have ever met.

Henry, never one to boast of his skills, is the best flycaster I have ever seen. I have watched nationally known flyrodders give casting

Henry Malone: Bruce Houck's guru and "one of the finest gentlemen I have ever met," according to the author. "The best flycaster I have ever seen."

demonstrations and describe their flycasting, but not one of these men could measure up to the abilities that Henry possessed. With one graceful backcast and just one apparently effortless forecast, Henry could propel 70 feet of line with a modest fiberglass flyrod. The graceful ease of Henry's casting was truly an art. I think the word *art* is often trivialized in respect to fly tying and fly-fishing, but you had to see Henry cast to appreciate his artistry. Even today, after thousands of hours of fly-fishing, I am still trying, unsuccessfully, to emulate Henry's elegant casting.

It was also during this early period of the 1970s that I began to read voraciously about fly-fishing — about its history, about the entomology of trout flies and patterns used to mimic real flies, and about the adventures of other anglers. The names of Flick, Fox, Marinaro, Schweibert, Traver, and Wright became deified in my mind. It was much less expensive for me to become acquainted with the writings of these noted anglers than it is for a modern neophyte. At the time, Crown Publishers, under the guidance of the well-known Nick Lyons, were reprinting many of the classic books about fly-fishing at affordable prices. In addition, *Field and Stream* magazine organized a book club that distributed these books. That I have obtained a modest fly-fishing library is due in large part to Crown Publishers and to the now-defunct Field and Stream Book Club.

These influential books led me to do a good bit of experimenting with my fly-fishing. Instead of fishing only from 6:00 or 6:30 in the evening until dark, I began to give mornings and even afternoons some serious consideration, though my summer quest for a master's degree interfered with the development of my early- and mid-day skills. However, the master's degree quest also led me, indirectly, to learn to fish with midges on a regular basis.

I had obtained a teaching job in Bellwood, Pennsylvania, after graduating from Lock Haven, and, as I often say, if I have to work for a living, I think teaching school is the way I like best to earn my living.

After my classes ended for the day at Penn State, I often ventured five or six miles to famous Fishermen's Paradise near Bellefonte. The trout there see thousands of anglers each year, and the rising trout, while not easily spooked by bankside anglers, can be maddeningly selective. They are particularly fussy about fly sizes.

Henry had showed Bruce how to tie a little grizzly-hackled midge that worked reasonably well on the educated trout of the Paradise, and after classes, I got a real education as I hounded the trout. On good afternoons, I sometimes caught and released seven or eight nice trout on the size 22 and 24 midges which were attached to 7X tippets that tested at barely one pound at the time.

The deep pool below the waterfall is a good spot for trout because they like to hold in such areas. (Photo courtesy Paul Tofte)

During those years, we made a lot of special trips to Fishermen's Paradise. Many of these adventures to Paradise were made during the dead of winter and in early spring, before the regular trout season opened in April. Dressed in our deer-hunting outfits, using hand-warmers to keep our hands warm enough to fish at all, we tested our skills against the tough Paradise trout. Bruce, Dan, and I used the grizzly midges Henry had showed Bruce to do the bulk of our fishing. Occasionally, on warmer days, Henry, who had more sense than we did, would drive over from his home in Milesburg and show us how to catch the finicky trout. But even on the colder days, with ice in our rod guides, our noses dripping like leaky faucets, and probably suffering from cases of hypothermia, we managed to take a few trout. After those early years, we have made fewer and fewer winter trips to fish: It just didn't seem like fun after awhile. We weren't the only crazy fishermen, though. My old fishing notebooks reveal that on most outings we shared Paradise with a hundred or more other anglers; it looked like the first day of trout season on a stocked trout stream.

I landed my largest trout of those early years while fishing the Paradise one summer afternoon after graduate classes. There was a pod of nice fish feeding near a weedbed below one of the Paradise jack dams, and I was working on them. Finally, after countless rejections, one of the trout sucked in the little grizzly, and I set the hook. He led me on a merry 20-minute tour of the many weedbeds in his pool before I gingerly netted him. He was an honest 18 inches long and remains one of the most memorable trout that I have caught. My weak-kneed responses to his powerful lunges are feelings I can still recall over 15 years later.

Though our adventures at Paradise are pleasant to recall, they are only a small fraction of our fishing adventures from the early 1970s. Bruce, Dan, and I fished as much as we could during those seasons, and we really became pretty educated fly-fishermen.

Our enthusiasm led us on many expeditions to north-central Penn-sylvania, where Bruce served as guide if Henry wasn't along. Our reading had led us to expand the selection of flies we toted along, and new (for us) patterns such as March Browns and Blue Quills proved their effectiveness on the trout of the north-central Pennsylvania freestone creeks.

I think what amazed us most was that good dry-fly fishing to heavy hatches of mayflies began on these creeks a good two to three weeks before the good dry-fly fishing normally commenced on our more southerly trout streams. Our home waters, while not true lime-stone spring creeks such as the Letort or Big Spring Creek, are spring-fed and have a different schedule of hatches than the northern frees-toners. For whatever reason, fly-fishing is usually slow around home until the second or third week of May most years, while the northern freestone waters are bursting with activity.

Names of these streams are unimportant: That they provided us and some of our friends with lots of exciting action is important. Also, while I may identify a few streams by name in this narrative, I do not want to be labeled a "kiss-and-tell fisherman."

Part of the enjoyment of fly-fishing is a spirited battle with a fish that's taken the fly but isn't yet netted.

The habits we developed during those years are ones that have stayed with us. Bruce likes the challenge of a tough-to-take trout and will stick with it until he catches it. He can be happy fishing in one pool during a two- to three-hour hatch. So can Dan, though he tends to be more like I am. When I am astream, I like to see what's around the next bend, and I can easily cover a mile or more of water in a couple hours of fishing, whether fishing to actively feeding trout or fishing to the water. My wanderlust astream has permitted me to find a lot of productive fishing holes over the years.

On the other hand, I have also been wandering around unproductive areas while Bruce or Dan has been latching onto large numbers of trout in a single pool. The funny thing is that by the end of most of our fishing outings together, we usually caught about the same number of trout. I am ashamed to admit, however, that Bruce or Dan generally landed the biggest trout of a trip while I was off gallivanting about.

Of these seasons, several things stand out. One is the flood of 1972. The entire spring of 1972 was a wet one. It rained every day or two, the fly hatches were sparse and appeared inconsistently, and the fly-fishing was pretty miserable. Finally, on June 22, things really hit the fan. The remains of Hurricane Agnes settled over Pennsylvania and dumped cloudfuls of water on the state. Picturesque rivers and creeks became raging torrents, causing about two billion dollars' worth of damage statewide. People lost their homes, and industries and businesses suffered terribly. Through it all, many people demonstrated great courage in the face of adversity.

One minor consequence of the flood was that I lost nearly two-thirds of a summer's fly-fishing education. The streams did not return to normal until August, though by early July I was back on the creeks, striving mightily to catch a few trout. I caught very few, as the trout, probably gorged during the high water, basically ignored the delayed hatches until August.

During the weeks of high water, I tried everything in my fly boxes. Darrell Claar, a fellow teacher, had been showing me how to fish streamers early that season, and I'd caught a few trout on them. One day in early July, while fishing a Silver Doctor streamer, I landed a 12-inch sucker. Some would say that the sucker was on the other end of the line.

The fishing really picked up in August. Some of June's fly hatches emerged during August and partially compensated for the lost hatches of June and early July. My persistence kept me astream during the autumn, too, and by the end of the 1972 season, I had caught more than 300 trout and was extremely impressed with myself.

Another memory from those years is a trip that Bruce and I made to the revered trout streams of the Catskill Mountains in New York during June 1973. On the trip we met a couple of our heroes, Walt Dette and Art Flick, who patiently and kindly tolerated our worship. Despite our rather unrefined skills, we managed to catch and release 125 trout in four days of fishing, a good tally for us at the time. Our trip would have been typical of many if it were not for an unusual experience on the big Beaverkill on our last evening there.

You have to picture this: Bruce and I were such neophyte, provincial anglers that we did not even own a pair of chest waders. Hip boots had always been sufficient on our small home creeks. And those hip boots were all we had with us. For those who are not familiar with the Beaverkill River downstream from the town of Roscoe, let it be known that hip boots don't get you more than a few feet away from the river's banks. Try as we might to stay dry, Bruce and I both managed to wade too far every day, and water poured into our boots, soaking us. Perhaps if we had been able to handle 50 feet of line. . .

Anyhow, on this evening we were dealing as effectively as we could with a heavy caddis hatch. The nearest match we had for the hatching caddisses were our trusty Adams: It was just before Leonard Wright's articles popularizing caddis imitations appeared in print. If the truth be told, I didn't even know the flies were caddisses; I only knew they didn't look a lot like my Adams. Even so, I was still managing to catch a few trout.

Fly-fishing gear includes waders or hip boots, a flyrod and flies. An angler is shown here "gearing up" for a day of fly-fishing.

It was nearly dark when I finally latched onto a trout that had been frustrating me all evening. He had been dimpling by a midstream rock, but I guessed from the heavy rings coming from his rises that he was a dandy.

My suspicions were pretty well confirmed after I finally hooked him and he tore off madly, making my reel scream in the fading light.

"Aha," I gloated to myself, "the biggest trout of the trip. He's gonna make Bruce's 16-incher look like a minnow."

But the battle wasn't won by gloating. The fish's mad dash took him out of the pool and into some rapid water below — a trick that trout rarely use on my small home creeks. Of course, being the innocent I was, I had no backing on my fly reel, and as the line melted away, I stumbled clumsily after the runaway trout.

"Oh, Lord! That's even colder after sunset!" I wailed as water poured in over the tops of both my hip boots as I attempted to prevent the powerful trout's escape.

"What are you doing, Rich?" yelled Bruce from the pool below. I could hardly hear him. "Got a big one on?"

"Yes!" I hollered back. "If I can get him settled down, can you net him for me when I get down to you?"

"Sure thing," Bruce called, wading to shore, putting his rod on the bank.

Meanwhile, the fish wasn't cooperating with me at all: He had reversed directions and had fought madly to get back to the pool he had left. I sloshed after him. This time I tripped along the edge of the riffles and fell, bloodying my left hand as I tried to break my fall. I lost what was then my "official fishing hat," a paisley pork pie hat that would have best been permanently lost instead of being retrieved by my loyal brother-in-law. Water saturated the few remaining dry areas of my fishing attire. I did manage to scramble back to my feet, and I was able to put enough tension on the line to turn the unruly trout before he got back into his home pool.

He sulked only briefly before zooming back down the river; acting much like a runaway locomotive.

"C'mon, Rich! Get him down here!" called Bruce encouragingly. "He's been on ten minutes. He ought to be getting tired!"

"Heck," I thought as I slogged after the trout as gracefully as I could with two boots full of water, "I hope so. *I'm* getting tired."

The fish continued on his merry way, finally leaving the rapids and entering Bruce's pool, 20 or 30 feet out from him. I arrived at the head of the pool shortly thereafter.

How big, Rich?"

"I dunno. I think he's bigger than the 18-incher I got at Paradise last year," I replied hopefully. "I don't want to screw up now."

I was shivering uncontrollably, both from the hypothermic effects of my waterlogged condition and from a bad case of frazzled nerves. I certainly didn't want to lose what was then my trout of a lifetime.

Suddenly the line went limp. The trout had escaped. No, wait! As I frantically reeled in line, I again felt a sharp tug as the trout renewed the battle, which was now going on 20 minutes or so.

"Hey fella, need a light?" a stranger called in the dark from above. "I know you've had that fish on for a long time, and my friend and I'd kind of like to see it."

"Sure," I replied shakily as the fish made a short run, and I turned my attention its way. "My brother-in-law is down there 10 or 15 yards, and he's gonna net it for me. If you'd help him with your flashlight, I'd sure appreciate it."

"No problem. We'll help you," the stranger kindly told me as he and his friend eased around me. "Hang on."

The trout, meanwhile, was rapidly tiring: His long runs had ended, and all he could do now was bore deeply as he tried to dislodge the hook. It was only a minute or two after the strangers had gone down to help Bruce that I could see the water sparkle as the fish splashed tiredly near the surface.

I held on tightly, backing out of the river, as I eased the fish toward the flashlight about 20 feet below me. Shortly afterwards, I felt the tautness go out of the line as Bruce netted the fish. "Got him?" I called in the darkness.

"Yeah, Rich, got him," Bruce replied, a little sardonically, I thought, as the light flicked off. There was a pause, a slight splash, and a little chuckling from the trio below me. How could they act that way at my moment of triumph?

"What's going on?" I called.

I heard a little mumbling as I stumbled down to the trio. When I arrived, I found that the strangers had gone on down the river. Only Bruce was there.

"Well, Rich, you sure got him. That was some battle," he said dryly.

"How big is he? Show him to me before we leave."

"You don't want to see him. Anyhow, I already released him"

"What? I . . . ." I began, kind of irritated, but also knowing that something wasn't quite right.

"Rich, that trout wasn't more than 14 inches long. You spent a half-hour playing a 14-inch trout. We lost all that fishing time while you played him."

"That's impossible. He had to be huge. Or," I thought suddenly between shivers, "he was foul-hooked."

Bruce began to laugh. "Sorry, Rich, he wasn't. He was hooked in the corner of his mouth. And he wasn't big either. Come on, let's get to the truck. We've got a six-hour drive ahead of us, and you have to get out of those wet clothes. Here's your hat, too. Boy, do you look ridiculous."

"All right," I replied dejectedly, again shaking like a quaking aspen leaf. "I can't believe it. That trout felt huge. I've caught enough trout to know he was a big one."

Bruce just chuckled, though when we finally climbed out of the river in the dark and prepared to leave for home, he told me that I'd better not tell anyone what had happened — especially about how I had spoiled the last half-hour of fishing for him and the two strangers. As I donned some dry clothes, I agreed that was a splendid idea. I did not want to acquire a reputation as a buffoon.

It was years before I mentioned this Beaverkill incident to anyone. I would not have related it at all, except that I think I know what happened that night. I recently read a John Taintor Foote tale called "The Diver Does His Stuff." That story's hero loses a giant trout and ends up landing a chub that takes the dislodged fly. I think that's what happened to me.

An angler works the Letort Spring Run in Pennsylvania.

At one point during my half-hour battle, I felt the line go slack and then tighten quickly. I'm pretty certain that I had had a lunker brown trout zooming around the Beaverkill with my fly in his mouth, as I sloshed to keep up with him. I figure that I lost him when the line went slack, and the 14-incher grabbed the dislodged fly.

What does Bruce have to say about this? Well, though he occasionally reminds me of the incident, I haven't yet told him what I think occurred. After all, he might be a little skeptical. But I am now positive that I really was attached to a monster brown trout on that long-ago evening on the Beaverkill.

Or, was I?

Anyhow, besides the trip to the hallowed Catskills, we also had to make a couple trips to the famous waters of Pennsylvania's Cumberland Valley. Besides reading the books of Fox and Marinaro, we had heard Marinaro speak at a banquet and had actually talked with him and his friend, Bill Fritz, afterwards. Both were congenial, and Fritz particularly urged us to visit the Cumberland Valley. "The Letort's tough," he told us, "but there are 'hogs' on Falling Spring that will make your heart pound."

Bruce and I made our first excursion to the Letort on a hot, mid-August day when all that hit were mosquitoes. By the end of the afternoon, we were both weary and irritable.

That initial foray was saved for us by a young angler we met as we were leaving the Letort. "Go to the Yellow Breeches this evening," he urged. "It has a hatch of White Millers that you won't believe."

We drove to Allenberry on the Breeches, and at dusk the flies appeared. It was a blizzard hatch and spinner fall of white mayflies that have become famous during the past decade. Our first encounter with *Ephoron lukon* was modest, each of us salvaging our day by catching and releasing a half-dozen chunky trout.

Bruce and I made several more trips to the Letort during the early 1970s. Normally, Dan went with us, and sometimes one or two of Bruce's friends would accompany us, too. After our inauspicious first adventure, things improved. We normally got into several trout apiece, and generally one of us would latch onto a trout of 17 or 18 inches. It was exhausting to pound the Letort for an entire day: Its soggy banks made movement difficult, and the hot, summer sun really drained our energy. We were all young then, though, and we thought this challenging fishing was great fun.

We also attended a couple of the Labor Day parties of the Letort regulars, quite by accident. I think every notable angler of the Cumberland Valley was at these bashes, held in what is now known as Marinaro's Meadow. Fox, Marinaro, expert angler Ed Shenk, and others sat around and told trout tales until the wee hours of the morning. It was all pretty heady stuff for a bunch of young, impressionable fly-fishermen, and the opinions of the Cumberland Valley anglers were gospel to us and certainly influenced the attitudes we still hold concerning fly-fishing for trout.

Chapter 3

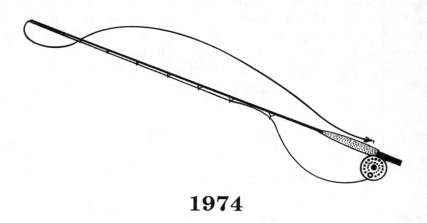

1974

The 1974 trout season was, without a doubt, the most instructive, intense season I've ever spent as a trout fisherman. It also nearly ruined fishing for me.

That season I had set a goal for myself of catching 1,000 trout during the regular trout season. I wanted to catch them all on flies. I had concluded the previous season with more than 500 trout to my credit, and I figured I could double that tally if I really worked at it.

At that time, Pennsylvania's trout season extended from mid-April to Oct. 31, and I knew that I couldn't have very many fishless outings if I were to accomplish my mission. I knew that I wanted to fish over trout that were relatively undisturbed and that would be willing to take a properly presented fly. This was in the days before the fish commission's Operation FUTURE program, a program that emphasized wild trout management, and even the best of Pennsylvania's wild trout streams were heavily stocked and drew hordes of meat-crazed maniacs early in the season. Consequently, I spent my early outings scouring small, fairly remote mountain brooks that were not pounded to death by the mad hordes. These little gems got me off to a creditable start, though in recent years I have discovered other little brooks that would have provided better action than I had in 1974. Even so, a gaudy Royal Coachman wet fly helped to account for more than 50 wild brook trout before I even set foot on the bank of a stream that had been stocked.

The April weather that year was wet and cold, and the local trout streams were running high and green with run-off. These conditions were not exactly favorable for fishing success, and on my home waters I was forced to rely on streamers fished slow and deep for sluggish trout. Most of the trout I caught on streamers took a size 10 Black-nosed Dace bucktail. The best April day was one I spent fishing to a Blue Quill hatch on a lovely north-central freestone creek. By May I had landed over 100 trout, and I was on my way.

May turned out to be a splendid fishing month. The local hatches of caddisses, craneflies, and Sulphurs each began about a week earlier than normal, helping my cause. Despite my job and taking one of my last graduate courses, I missed fishing only two days in May. I fished under all kinds of conditions: rain, cold, heat, and wind. But for most of the month, the weather was good, never muddying the streams as is often the case. Without going into a day-by-day account of the month's angling, suffice it to say that by the end of the month I had tallied 386 trout, all from public-access waters. On my most productive day, I caught and released 35 eight- to 12-inch brown trout as caddisses, craneflies, and a few small mayflies emerged over a three-hour period.

The fishing never tailed off. During the summer I had to take two graduate courses and write my master's paper. I took a rainy day, threw a few things together, and completed the paper by the end of the day. That just shows you the quality of my master's paper. Except for a few courses at the Altoona branch campus of Penn State, the things I did to obtain a master's degree were inane exercises. The final two graduate courses were typical of most of the ones I took, and I didn't have to work very hard to pass them. I was able to be on my favorite trout streams nearly every day for three months.

The discovery of a couple decent *Tricorythodes* hatches on trout streams not too far from home allowed me to fish over actively feeding fish, but the real boon to my fish-taking ability was my discovery of the effectiveness of Leonard Wright's wonderful Fluttering Caddis. Wright advocated fishing his caddis with a "sudden inch" of movement, but I found that these jaunty flies worked perfectly well when fished dead drift. A size 14 Wright Caddis became my favorite fly for fishing the water during midsummer, and it remains my favorite stream prober to this day. Though I did not enjoy the intense, spectacular success that I enjoyed while fishing to the hatches of late spring and early summer, I had landed 927 trout before I returned to work in the autumn.

During the final two months of the season, my fishing time was seriously curtailed. I was the school's cross country coach, and I did

The author proudly admits, "I gloat when I land a brown trout such as this one."

not fish at all during 35 of the 61 days of September and October. Many of the evenings I did get to fish were of the 30- to 45-minute variety, too. Even so, I caught my thousandth trout on Sept. 28.

I wish I could say it was the two-foot monster of my dreams, but it wasn't. It was a modest 12-inch wild brown garbed in his resplendent spawning attire.

When the season ended a month later, I had landed 1,094 trout during the regular open season. If I added the 24 trout I caught at Paradise during my two days of fishing there in March, my total would be 1,118 trout during 1974. That is really a pretty impressive season for someone who I now realize was not a very skillful fly-fisherman.

This tally of fish was possible because of my extreme persistence, favorable fishing conditions, and a lack of real responsibilities. Being a bachelor for the last summer of my fishing career, I could fish anytime I wanted to, and I could travel to any place I could afford to go during the summer. It was really a very favorable situation.

During the mid-April to Oct. 31 trout season, I fished 151 of the 211 days. Some of the 60 days I did not fish were due to inclement weather, and the others were work-related. I figured that this was the equivalent of two lost months of fishing.

Many times I fished both during the morning and in the evening as I sought to attain my objective. I also fished during intense rains and during 90-degree heat waves. At the time, I thought of this as dedication to the sport, but I realize now that I made hard work out of my sport. It is a wonder that this work did not spoil fly-fishing for me forever. Truthfully, I was glad when the end of October arrived and I did not *have* to fish any more that year.

Despite my making work out of fishing, the 1974 season was without a doubt the most instructive of all my trout fishing seasons. I seriously cataloged the hatches on my favorite streams, and this has helped me to enjoy replays of previously successful adventures.

I also began to pay more serious attention to water temperature and how it affects fishing success. Briefly, I realized that the closer the water temperature was to 63 to 64 degrees, the more trout that I caught. This generally occurred in the morning on most of the streams I fish. Only lately have I realized that Leonard Wright's maxim of "the closer and the faster the water temperature approaches the trout's optimum, the more actively they feed," is true on the creeks I fish. I think I realized this intuitively, but only recently did I overtly acknowledge why morning and evening are good trout fishing times in midsummer. But, even in 1974, I looked for water temperatures in the 60 to 68 degree range. When I hit water of 70 degrees or warmer, I generally fished elsewhere.

I also avoided areas that Dan had labeled as "Chubvilles." By summer, the trout in these unshaded, degraded sections of creek disappeared, no doubt migrating to spring holes. Had I spent any appreciable amounts of time in these areas that harbor only chubs and other non-game fish, I would never have attained my goal.

I discovered that certain fly patterns were helpful. I have already noted the importance of the Wright Caddis to my fishing. I also found fly patterns that worked well for me during the Sulphur hatches and spinner falls. I began to recognize the importance of imitating several stages of a mayfly's life cycle, and I came up with emerging nymph patterns, dun patterns, and a deadly spinner fly to use during the hatches I fish, especially the Sulphurs. In addition, I experimented with wet flies and streamers early in the day.

I became convinced that the trout of summer and autumn are opportunistic feeders and are generally less particular about fly styles than they are when they are locked onto a hatch. The major exception to this, of course, is the small flies that are needed to duplicate the summer-hatching *Tricorythodes* mayflies. The Wright Caddis, my favorite stream prober, probably doesn't imitate just one bug during the summer. Rather, I think it is effective because its silhouette resembles that of many insects, from small grasshoppers to katydids. I think the effectiveness of the ubiquitous Adams and some of its variations can be explained similarly.

It was about this time I became convinced that how I dressed contributed to the number of trout I caught, too. Like many beginning anglers, I had become enamored of fancy gear and trinkets advertised in the fly-fishermen's dream books. However, the light, bright colors of this gear allowed the trout to see me coming. I began to dress in subdued colors: dark green particularly. I exchanged my Joe Orvis hat for a camouflage cap. I think that these items, particularly on small creeks in late summer when the streams are low and clear, help me to avoid frightening skittish trout.

I also learned to rely on my fishing journal. Though my friend Gary "Mooch" Irvin teases me about my keeping of copious notes, these notes led me to fish certain places on specific dates in 1974. That I was able to repeat previous successes was due, in part, to reviewing my notes regularly.

How about this rainbow trout caught on a size 22 Trico?

One thing I did not do in 1974 that I really like to do now was "play Columbus." As Bob Mingle, my father-in-law, likes to say, "Columbus took a chance," but I couldn't take many chances on exploring new water if I wanted to catch 1,000 trout. Consequently, I fished familiar water almost every day and really did not discover any new sections of productive water. In the long run, it was a major error, especially on the Little Juniata River, which is only about 20 minutes from my home. At the time, the Little Juniata was in the fourth or fifth year of its recovery from severe industrial pollution.

Huge trout were being caught there regularly, and it wasn't being pressured as badly as it was only a year later after it received a great deal of local, regional, and national publicity. 1974 was probably the best year for catching large trout on the river, and I missed out on it. Even though the river remains a good place to fish for trout in the eight- to 12-inch range, it sadly does not harbor anywhere near the number of trophy trout it once did and probably still could. Overpublicity and overkilling of its trout have contributed to the dreadful decline of the Little Juniata as a trophy trout stream. Though movements are afoot to establish some kind of catch-and-release regulations on the river, the social aspects of catch-and-kill that now exist on the lovely stream will be difficult for fishery managers to deal with.

My largest trout of 1974 was a sleek 18-inch brown that I landed on a fur ant on the legendary Letort on Labor Day weekend. However, I discovered a group of spawners one October Sunday afternoon that dwarfed this fine trout: I tried unsuccessfully all afternoon to catch one of these half-dozen large trout.

Because 20 inches was the minimum size for keepers on Pennsylvania's Fish-for-Fun areas at the time, Bruce, Dan, and I were obsessed with landing a 20-inch trout for the wall. Since I had been living in Bellwood for a while now, 35 minutes from home and these trout, and was still coaching, I couldn't pursue the trout the next day. I knew Dan could fish on Monday; so I called him that evening and explained the situation. "You'd better get after them. I don't know where they came from, but they won't stay there long," I told him.

The next evening I received a call at my apartment. It was Dan.

"Well, did you get the big one?" I asked him.

"No," he told me, "it just cruised around like it did to you yesterday."

"Didn't you get any of them?"

"Well, I got one. Boy, Rich, he's a dandy. He's about 21 inches and weighs over four pounds. He's going on the wall! I got him in the deep pool by the evergreen at about 9:00 this morning. I saw him lying in the shallows; so I pitched him a size 12 cricket, and he sucked it right in."

"You got him on a dry fly?"

"Yes, sir!"

"Boy, I'll bet he gave you some fight."

"Not as much as you'd think. I imagine it only took me five minutes to land him. He never left the pool."

The next weekend I got to admire Dan's fine trout. It was indeed a local lunker, probably even more special than we then realized. When the Pennsylvania Fish Commission conducted stream census surveys a few years later under their Operation FUTURE program, only one trout of 20 inches was found in any of their stops on our local creeks. Dan's trout was certainly a unique fish.

Dan's trout was special to all of us. Though Dan, Bruce, and I have all caught a few trout of 20 inches or better since that time, Dan's was the first. At the time, we all possessed only rudimentary fishing skills and modest tackle, and catching the big trout under those handicaps was much more difficult than landing a similar fish is for us with the gear and experience we have today.

I once wrote a magazine article, "One Thousand Trout." In that piece I wrote that catching 1,000 trout is not all fun, that you must take your fishing seriously. Though I still take my fishing pretty seriously, I never again wish to become obsessed with numbers. In 1974 I was astream at times I would really have preferred to be doing other things: swimming or just plain relaxing. I was fishing because I had to, not because I wanted to, and there's a big difference. Though I have caught 1,000 or more trout numerous times since 1974, I never did it again due to goal setting. It was a result of favorable conditions, accumulated knowledge, and good luck while fishing only about half as often as I did in 1974.

Though setting goals to catch large numbers of trout is something I no longer do (in fact, I no longer keep a running tally of the number I catch during a season), 1974 remains a benchmark year for me as a fly-fisherman. I worked hard to accomplish a goal, but more importantly, I learned that I could catch fish consistently over an entire season while using only flies. I have never again drowned a worm in hopes of catching a trout.

Chapter 4

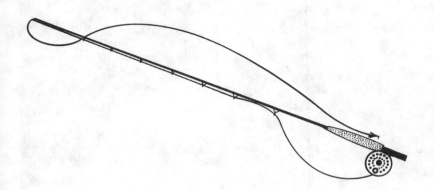

HOLIER THAN THOU?

As I delved into the writings of the luminaries of the world of fly-fishing, I realized that the doctrine of catch-and-release fishing for trout was a common thread. The authors' insistence that catch-and-release fishing was necessary to maintain healthy fisheries was justified in a variety of ways, from the biological to the aesthetic to the social. I absorbed so much of this preaching that I became a convert to what I felt was a holy cause.

Even in my formative years as a flyrodder, I had released many trout. I had decided that trout under 10 inches weren't worth keeping, that a fish under that size wasn't going to make much of a meal. In addition, when the woman who dumped me told me that trout were too pretty to kill, I began to appreciate the true loveliness of wild trout. As I encountered the argument that released trout are going to grow into larger fish, I selfishly acknowledged that bopping 14- or 15-inch trout on the noggin was going to prevent them from ever becoming the elusive 20-incher of my dreams. For a lot of what I thought were pretty good reasons, I completely quit killing the trout that I caught. Heck, I even refused to keep even one or two stocked trout for my own mother, who enjoyed a meal of fresh trout on occasion. "Buy 'em at the store," I'd tell her.

My fishing journals from the late 1970s and early 1980s are filled with nasty remarks about fishermen who kept a trout or two. "Joe

Many fly-fishermen believe in catch-and-release fly-fishing. Here the author is shown preparing to release a nice brown trout.

'Killer' Schmoe was on the creek this evening," I penned. "He killed the two trout he caught. Boy, what a rotten guy."

"Wyatt Burp was fishing in Blackwell's Meadow. If he keeps killing the trout he catches, there soon won't be many left," was another typical entry.

I even became so bold as to confront fellows who were killing trout and tell them that they were ruining the trout fishing by their actions. I condemned their lack of sportsmanship. I criticized their lack of ethics. I probably even insulted their family tree on occasion. It's a wonder I have any teeth left: These guys had every right to punch my lights out.

I became a real crusader. So did my fishing cohorts. We seemed to believe it was a mortal sin to kill a noble trout.

We weren't too far off base either, especially about streams that will support larger numbers of trout than they do. I have heard biologists admit that angler harvest is the limiting factor in having trophy populations of fish on many creeks. Enthusiastic anglers in my bailiwick recognize the Little Juniata River as a case in point. Many believe that if catch-and-release regulations or slot limits of some sort were established on the little river that it could again develop into a trophy trout fishery. I am one of the believers.

A little creek not too far from the Little Juniata supports a healthy population of wild brown trout and has not been stocked for a number of years now. Over the years, its trout population has increased in most areas, as the biologists had predicted when it was decided to quit stocking it. However, populations of trout in its hardest-fished sections are not as good as they should be, and trout overharvest is probably the cause. Had slot limits or special regulations been adopted, the little creek would have been able to support the additional larger trout that the biologists told us it could. But serious objections from local fishermen dictated that even though stocking was to be discontinued, the bopping on the noggin of any seven-inch trout, up to eight of them per day, would remain in effect. If it were protected as a few other Pennsylvania trout waters are, its trout population and the size of its fish could rival the best of them. I am one who believes that trout in creeks such as this one deserve and need protection as human pressures on our wild resources continue to increase.

However, I am not as sanctimonious about keeping a trout or two as I once was. I believe my holier-than-thou attitude was a real turn-off to other sportsmen, and when I read the verbal battles in today's fly-fishing magazines, I realize that a crusading, self-righteous attitude is often counterproductive in trying to get others to kill fewer trout.

41

This trying attitude makes other anglers defensive, and they insist that they'll kill all the fish they want.

In addition, there are some creeks where it makes sense to harvest the trout that are caught. Streams that overheat in summer, where the trout will die from thermal stress, are examples. One such stream comes to mind. Canoe Creek in central Pennsylvania was once a viable wild trout stream. It was productive enough that it was under consideration for classification as an unstocked wild trout stream. However, a few years back, the local game warden stocked a family of beavers in the creek's middle reaches. The ponds the beavers built contributed to the overheating of Canoe Creek's water. During a follow-up study to classify Canoe Creek as a wild trout stream, the fish commission team came up with few wild trout — but did discover a growing population of little pickerel! Though the fish commission and the local Trout Unlimited chapter tried to have the beavers removed, the creek flows through gamelands, and the powers-that-be decided that the beavers would stay. In a stream such as present-day Canoe Creek, which now boasts a population of stocked trout that will probably die from the thermal stresses of midsummer, there is nothing wrong with taking trout for the frying pan. Though I do not fish there much anymore, I still release the trout I catch on Canoe Creek, vainly hoping that they will somehow reestablish populations of wild trout.

Are we catch-and-release flyrodders really correct that wild trout ought to be released to fight again? Yes. In streams that can biologically support larger numbers and grow larger trout than they now do, catch-and-release options or slot limits are management tools that ought to be used. However, on waters that are marginal and where the trout will suffer and die from stress, management emphasizing the taking of trout is practical.

Chapter 5

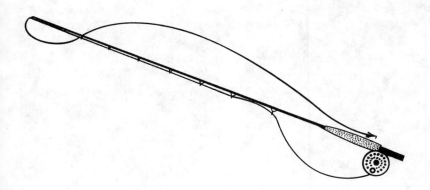

MARRIAGE

During the fall of 1974, I began dating the woman who knocked me off my feet. It began innocently enough.

I was sitting in a local beer garden one evening with Bruce and another friend when my wife-to-be walked past us on her way to the restaurant in the next room. "Hi, Rich" she smiled.

"Hi," I managed to return, despite my rather disoriented condition.

"Who was that?" asked my friend. "She's a pretty nice-looking girl."

"That was Donna Mingle," I stammered. "Yeah, she's awfully pretty, all right. She's the girls' basketball coach in town and teaches grade school."

"Why don't you ask her out?" both Bruce and my friend remarked, more of a command than a question. These two were married, and I figured that theirs was a "misery loves company" type of attitude.

"Trout season's not over," I expounded. "I don't have time to be running around with women while the trout season is in. Catching trout is a lot more important than chasing women is. Maybe I'll ask her out after trout season ends."

"You're crazy, Rich. You ought to march back to the restaurant and ask her for a date right now," Bruce said. Bruce was more than a mere brother-in-law; he was a super friend, a fact that it took me a lot of years to realize.

The author's wife is very understanding of her husband's hobby. Tate says that after 15 years of marriage, "Donna still handles the fishing and me with toleration and love."

Barroom talk, as most people know, is cheap, and I continued to defend myself in a variety of beer-influenced manners. I didn't work up the courage to ask Donna out for several weeks. In fact, one of my cousins who taught with her did it for me.

As most guys who have been burnt in the court of love, I was quite wary about getting involved in another love relationship. Though I dated fairly regularly during the winters and occasionally at other times, the truth is that I still hurt over being rejected.

I struggled valiantly to cover up my hurt. I really threw myself into my teaching career, and my interest in fly-fishing and fly tying became more of an obsession than a hobby. I insisted that I didn't have time to date regularly when really I was afraid to fall in love again. When Donna entered my life, she had to overcome the many defenses I used to keep from being hurt again.

Well, one date led to another and to another, and before long it was April: trout season. In previous years, if I was still dating in April, I abruptly stopped, but this year even I knew things were different. My mother was really vocal about it.

"Richard," she told me every time she saw me, "Donna has really changed you. You're a lot nicer and more considerate than you used to be. She is really good for you."

Of course, I denied this, insisting that I had not changed in any way whatsoever. But even with the approach of trout season, I knew I wanted to keep seeing Donna. Though I guess I knew I'd fallen in love with her, I was still too unsure of myself to declare it. As I look back, I am truly amazed at the patience she showed with me as our relationship developed.

When trout season arrived, she urged me to head for the creeks. Though she would go along on occasion, she told me that she would rather let me fish alone, that we could share our special times later. What was even more amazing is that I found myself willing to give up weekend fishing time to date. My defenses were crumbling.

I think the walls I had surrounded myself with totally crashed one Friday evening in late May. I had driven home to see her and to fish to a Sulphur hatch. When I'd left her house to hit the creek, I must've said something incredibly stupid. She told me later that she worried until dark that I was angry with her. I wasn't. I was just anxious to fish to the Sulphurs, which were at the peak of their cycle on the little creeks I favor. Anyhow, after a successful evening on the creek, fishing until long after nightfall, I arrived in triumph back at her house. I could see that she was shaken.

"What's wrong?" I had the temerity to ask.

"Don't you know?"

"No."

"I was worried about you. After you left, I wasn't sure you were coming back. I was afraid you were going to some tavern someplace."

"What?" I began.

"I even called your mother. If you hadn't gotten back here by 10:30, we were going to come looking for you. We were going to look in all the bars around until we found you."

"Why were you going to do that?" I asked. I suppose I even laughed at the thought of my girlfriend and my mother searching for me in some of the dives in the area.

"It's not funny, Richard. I thought you were angry when you left, and I know you used to spend a lot of time in bars. I don't want that to happen to you again. I won't let it happen! You're too important to me."

I was shocked. No one outside my immediate family had ever said anything like that to me before. Looking back, I guess it's sort of an odd way for my defenses to have shattered, but if I hadn't known before, I surely did at this time that Donna cared for me the way I was, not the way she hoped I would become.

Things happened rapidly after that, and Donna agreed to marry me. By the end of summer we were married, and I moved back to my hometown to establish our home. This all occurred in less than a year, mind you.

Fly-fishing runs in the family. The author's son, Bobby, concentrates on tying a fly.

I'm really not sure what redeeming qualities Donna found in me, but I know I'm fortunate to have her for my wife. She has helped me through some personal crises, tolerated all the faults I've had — smoking, chewing tobacco which I substituted for smoking until I managed to give it up too, and more — and has really encouraged me

46

to enjoy my hobbies, even at the expense of some time we could be sharing. Heck, when trout season approaches, she often prods me to do a little early fishing at Paradise or one of the other year-around trout fisheries not too far from home. "You're acting like a grumpy old bear. Go fishing so that you'll be bearable around here," she'll say.

It is advice I sometimes take when my woodcutting is caught up. Marriage has truly affected my development as a fly-fisherman. No longer do I want (have) to fish everyday. Instead, I choose times that I think will provide favorable fishing, preferring to spend some of my time with Donna and my son, Bobby. Even so, I'm still pretty fanatical about my fly-fishing, averaging somewhere between 75 and 90 days of fly-fishing each year. Of course, I don't fish all day any longer. I average about two hours per trip, a length of time Donna seems to think is acceptable.

Was I lucky? You can bet your ranch on it. Being the non-fishing wife of a fly-fishing fanatic is no picnic, and being married to a moody one is even tougher. After 15 years of marriage, Donna still handles the fishing and me with toleration and love.

Chapter 6

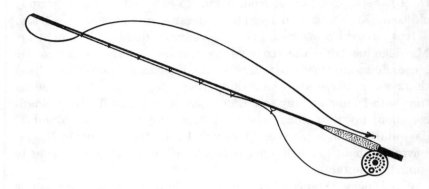

"THE WEIRD GUYS"

As I spent increasing amounts of time on the stream, I began to encounter familiar faces. There was Michael "Pike" DiBartolome, a skillful, solitary live bait fisherman who was a local legend for his ability to bring home large trout. He was often astream at daybreak and after dark in his quest for local lunkers. Though regarded as secretive and reticent, he shared some of his secrets with me after I got to know him. I was able to successfully apply these secrets to my fly-fishing.

There were the Johnstown "meat" fishermen, as my friends and I called them in our sanctimonious days. These were a group of skillful bait fishermen who used live crickets with deadliness to fill their creels with trout. I now realize that catch-and-release angling was not the ethic when they learned to fish, and though their full baskets still seem excessive to me, I recognized that their fishing was an escape from the drudgery and danger of their jobs in Johnstown's steel mills, which were a powerful industrial force until the early 1970s.

There were others, too, and as I recall, they were almost all live bait fishermen. However, there were a couple exceptions to this, a couple guys I refer to as "the weird guys." I suppose this sounds nasty, but I don't intend it to be nasty: I just thought these men were unusual, so I dubbed them "the weird guys."

The first was a character of my formative days as a flyrodder.

I first met him during the summer of one of my early years on the stream. He favored two or three spots on a local creek I am going to call the Little Shawnee Creek from this point forward. The Little Shawnee is not a spectacular stream by most standards. Nowhere does its width exceed 35 feet. None of its pools are deeper than four feet, though a few banks are undercut incredibly far. Much of it flows through open pastures, overheating the water for trout. In many places it has eroded and continues to erode badly, and after summer rains, the water can stay silted for weeks. Yet a number of miles of the Little Shawnee and the small branch of the Shawnee are shaded and are fed by cold, life-sustaining springs. These areas support populations of wild brown trout. Though it took me a good many years to acknowledge, the Little Shawnee doesn't harbor a lot of large trout.

When I was young and read of all the 20-inchers that other fellows caught on their favorite waters, I couldn't understand why I couldn't catch them on the Shawnee. But Pike DiBartolome and other more experienced fisherman helped me to understand that these trout were rare and were very special on the Shawnee. Later, the fish commission's stream surveys supported the veterans' assertions. Despite their rarity, there are a few lunkers here and there to quicken an angler's pulse. You can call me selfish if you choose, but the Little Shawnee is not the real name of this creek. However, the ecosystem and the wild trout population of the little creek are vulnerable enough that I feel obligated to protect it from over-exploitation in my writings.

Anyhow, this first "weird guy" was a nondescript-looking, middle-aged man, perhaps five feet seven or eight inches tall and weighing 130 pounds. He was shocked to see me as I rounded a bend in the stream as he was casting to a feeding trout.

"Good heavens, boy. Where did you come from?" he blurted out. I can still see the surprise in his eyes that were magnified by thick-lensed, wire rimmed glasses.

"Just down the creek," I replied. "You're fly-fishing?"

"Yes. I really love to fly-fish."

"I've never met you before. You are sure a fine caster."

He was, too. The small man cast softly and effortlessly. Casting-wise, he was a minor league version of Henry Malone. Though tolerant of me, I could tell that he regarded me as an intruder. Invariably when we met on the Little Shawnee, he asked me which direction I was fishing so that we could progress in opposite directions. "I don't want to interfere with your fishing," he would say each time. I knew what he really meant. It is a ploy I still use when I encounter other anglers on small streams.

I wouldn't say that we ever became friends, but after I discovered him watching me catch and release a trout late one summer evening, we began to exchange pleasantries on a regular basis. He revealed small bits about himself over a rather long period of time. For one, he never fished until June. "I don't like crowds. I think fishing is something to get you away from large numbers of people. There are just too many people on the stream early in the season for me. After bass season begins (about mid-June), the casual trout fishermen are gone, especially the ones who have to kill every trout they catch."

"But you miss out on the main fly hatches," I reminded him.

"Yes, but I'm willing to forego the hatches to be able to enjoy my fishing time. During the hatches, there are still too many guys on the creek for me to enjoy myself."

When he told me that, I began to think of him as "the weird guy." I couldn't understand how any fly-fishing addict could give up fishing during the major fly hatches when trout are most vulnerable to a fly-rodder's skills.

I thought his manner of dress was unusual, too. The man always wore a large straw hat, and on occasion he wore a tie, too! In my mind I regarded these accoutrements as odd and thought of the man as odd, too. He was probably a true gentleman. The hat? It was probably a fine sunscreen.

He proved to be a benefactor to my fly-fishing development, too. One evening when I was being absolutely humiliated by the trout, I ran into him. After exchanging greetings, he told me he'd been enjoying a fine evening of fishing. I had to ask, miserably, "What are you using?"

"A Badger Bivisible. Take one," and he offered his fly box. I gratefully accepted a fly, and after we went our opposite ways, I knotted on the large, feathery creation. It saved the evening for me as I caught several decent trout. The Badger fly is one I still carry with me to use on those difficult days when the trout are tough. Though it does not always produce, it accounts for enough trout for me to remain confident in it.

Although we never shared personal things — I never even asked the man his name — I suspect that he was a man defeated by diffidence, that solitary fly-fishing was his way of proving his self-worth. When he disappeared from the local fishing scene in the mid-1980s, I felt rather badly and missed our brief encounters. Though I remained on the lookout for him for a couple of seasons, I finally had to conclude that his fly-fishing days had ended.

50

The second of the two "weird guys" was a large, robust character who appeared on the Little Shawnee in the early 1980s and abruptly vanished after only three or four years of fishing. I dubbed him the "big, weird guy" the first time I ever saw him. I was fishing my way upstream one May evening during a flush hatch and spinner fall of Sulphurs. The trout were going nuts, and I was doing well. I wanted to end my evening at a deep pool below a little backroad bridge. As I approached the pool, I heard excited, ecstatic male giggling. "My gosh, what's that?" I wondered aloud.

As I arrived at the tail of the pool, I could see a large figure in the gloaming, playing what appeared to be a fine trout. The excited giggling was his. I quickly exited the stream and headed for my parked Scout. I noted his car, which was parked right behind my old, reliable fish vehicle, then left. I certainly wanted to avoid areas where I'd see that car in the future. I didn't want a guy like that fouling up my fishing! Imagine: laughing absurdly while fighting a fish. It wasn't normal. (That I occasionally talk to trees, flowers, birds, and trout while I'm fishing is perfectly acceptable, however.)

I couldn't really avoid bumping into this man on the Little Shawnee: It's a small stream, and parking places are limited in some sections. Inevitably, we began to exchange greetings, but with this man, I was the reticent one. He really liked to talk about fly-fishing, having only recently taken it up and being obsessed with learning as much about it as he could. He had equipped himself in the finest gear, had read all he could about the sport, was a disciple of catch-and-release angler-writers, and had even attended a couple of expensive fly-fishing schools. He was now learning to apply the ideas he had been exposed to, and I seemed to serve as his sounding board. I actually believed that he looked for my old Scout so that he could ask my opinions about his newest discoveries. The big fellow was really enthusiastic about fly-fishing, and on more than one occasion I parted with a dry fly or two to help him deal with an evening's dilemma.

This man, unlike the first one, seemed to like to talk about his personal life: a nasty divorce, a stressful management job, and how he handled things. I was sometimes uncomfortable listening to him talk, but remembering some of the problems I'd had dealing with a broken heart, I tried not to be rude when I excused myself from non-fishing conversations.

He drove flashy, expensive cars and regularly mentioned money matters. He was in an extreme hurry to "get into fly-fishing," as he noted, but also seemed to be obsessed by its many wonderful qualities.

At any rate, the "big, weird guy" was an interesting figure on the Little Shawnee during the early 1980s, and when I ceased to encounter him, I kind of missed him.

Truthfully, even though I prefer to fish alone most of the time, I looked forward to seeing "the weird guys." They were certainly not typical characters on the streams I like to fish, and I still miss their unusual perspectives about fly-fishing.

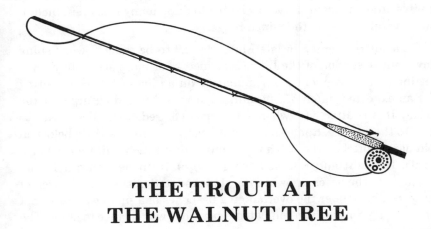

Chapter 7

THE TROUT AT
THE WALNUT TREE

After Dan had landed the 21-inch brown trout in 1974, my obsession with landing a similar trout increased. Even though Pennsylvania Fish Commission surveys of my local trout havens revealed that there were few such trout in my bailiwick, Dan's trout had proved that the few that were around could be caught — and caught on dry flies, though I would have been perfectly satisfied with a 20-incher caught on any style fly.

Although my skills greatly increased as the decade of the 1980s arrived, I had still failed to land a 20-inch trout. Sure, I had come close. I had managed several trout less than an inch shy of the magical 20 inch length. Most of these trout came from streams I traveled to, but after my marriage and the Arab oil embargo, my traveling in quest of trout diminished. Truthfully, I was perfectly satisfied with the fishing available to me within a half-hour of home, and even today, I spend 90 to 95 percent of my fishing time on local streams.

The 1981 season arrived with a bang. Its first several weeks were among the best weeks of fishing I had ever experienced on the small bucolic trout streams I frequent. These creeks, which sometimes become roiled and stay that way for weeks after heavy rains, had remained unsullied. The mayfly hatches had commenced earlier and had been much heavier than they normally are. Since I was making a conscientious effort to be a good husband and a reliable father for my young son, I had fished somewhat less often than I had during some previous seasons, though a couple of my neighbors suggested that I ought to be sued for divorce on grounds of desertion. During my forays after the trout, I had been able to dupe many fine ones, including several in the 17- to 18-inch range.

On a sultry evening in late May, May 29 to be exact, I was fishing my favorite section of the Little Shawnee — or more accurately I was sitting on a convenient log, ruminating on a plug of tobacco, waiting for an expected hatch of Sulphurs to arouse the feeding urges of the trout. It was after 8:00 when a few pale-colored little flies began to pop to the surface. Some small trout began to feed in a riffle below an old dam. I pitched the fish a tan comparadun which imitated the naturals. I caught and released the group of 10-inchers in quick succession. As the hatch grew heavier, I meandered upstream in search of bigger game. Under the overhanging branches of a small walnut tree, I spied heavy rings which indicated a big trout was surface feeding. The water between the trout and me was slow-moving with sinuous ribbons of current. I knew that I would have to wade 10 or 12 feet into the stream in order to get a drag-free float of my fly over the fish. The stream had not yet reached its midsummer low level, and by wading cautiously, I was able to avoid sending any shock waves over the actively feeding fish.

As I lengthened line with a series of false casts, I noted that the trout's feeding station was not more than an inch from a large rock on the streambank opposite me. There were several fronds of grass dangling into the water, which would make it difficult to obtain a proper presentation of my fly. When I had worked out enough line to drop my fly over the trout, I released my cast, and the fly fell an inch or two behind the trout's position.

However, the local trout had been kind to me all season, and this one swirled and greedily grabbed my fraud. I quickly set the hook and felt the solid resistance a fine fish gives. Almost immediately the fish sank to the bottom in an attempt to dislodge the hook, but the little hook held, and I believed that I had the situation well in hand.

The trout's next maneuver was to zip upstream toward a midstream rock, but for some reason he stopped short and returned downstream. When he reached the location where I had hooked him, he halted, came to the top, and attempted to roll on my tippet. Having had fish in prior seasons escape by using this trick, I had learned to lift my rod parallel to the stream's surface in order to keep the line away from a fish's roll. I quickly employed the tactic. As the trout rolled, I saw him. He was a dream fish, much larger, I felt, than any of the big trout

54

I had caught earlier in the season. He had to be the 20-incher of my dreams.

You can only imagine how I felt when the hook pulled loose. I did not know whether to curse or to cry as the fish slowly sank out of sight. Actually, as I recall, I just stood there in midstream, uttering not a sound, transfixed by what had occurred. Long afterwards, probably only a couple of minutes (though it seemed to be a lot longer), I realized that the trout was gone. I trudged back to my old Scout and exchanged my fishing togs for my street clothes and vowed that I would return to the meadow to catch the trophy trout which had defeated me that evening.

I spent the next four evenings in the meadow, fishing for small fries until nearly dark and then watching for "my" big one. But he did not show himself, and I gloomily concluded that he had either given up dining on mayflies or that he had left his home after our brief encounter. By the end of the week, I thought that the situation was at least temporarily hopeless, and I began to fish other sections of the creek while trying to forget about the fine trout.

In early June, the weather caught up with me and muddied the stream, rendering it unfishable. When the creek finally began to clear, I decided to fish bucktails in the now milky-colored water, thinking that perhaps the large trout would enjoy a sizable meal. Shortly after daybreak one crisp mid-June morning, I sallied forth to the meadow and fished a Black-nosed Dace pattern through the little stream's pools, riffles, and eddies. I tried several casts into the lair of the big trout, but there was no strike forthcoming. I had to be satisfied with catching the few small fish I managed to deceive. Though I was discouraged, I was not ready to concede final defeat to the trout.

My retreat from the meadow lasted only until early July, which was unseasonably cool. One afternoon while my son was napping and my wife was working, she urged me to go fishing (to get me out from underfoot, no doubt). I drove out to the creek, hoping for a little action fishing to the water. There was a definite absence of activity until I arrived at the walnut tree. Instead of one, there were two fish surface feeding. Since I could see no insects splatting into the water from the tree, I opted to employ my favorite summertime dry fly — a size 14 Wright Caddis.

The water retained enough flow to permit me to approach the trout without frightening them. I cast to the nearer fish first. He did not hesitate as he accepted my caddis, but I pulled too soon and succeeded in merely pricking him. He, by good fortune, was not the large trout I had previously lost — though he was a fine one, appearing to be in the 15-inch category.

His brief flirtation with my fly did not disturb his crony, who had continued to rise. After I had calmed myself and had checked to be sure that I still had a sharp point on my fly hook, I cast to the second fish. When he rose and inhaled my fly, I could see that he was the trout I was hoping to find: His broad back seemed to take forever to part the water's surface, and when I lifted my rod to set the hook, I encountered the log-like resistance I had felt in late May when I had first hooked him. This time, though, the battle was brief: The trout sank to the bottom, shook his head several times, and quickly dislodged the fly. The entire episode took no more than five seconds, but I was a nervous wreck as I shakily waded to shore, knowing full well that an angler is seldom accorded a second opportunity to capture a dream fish.

As I finished out the afternoon, I recalled Santiago, the hero of Ernest Hemingway's classic story *The Old Man and the Sea,* who, despite loving the great marlin he battled for three days, vowed to kill it. Like Santiago, I vowed to kill this trout, which had thus far proved to be my superior. Despite my catch-and-release fishing methods, I felt I deserved a trout for the wall. True, this was an exceptionally unusual fish, surviving to reach this size in a creek where a 14-inch trout is a large one, and he had really earned his right to survive. Despite this, my predatory instincts won out, and the contest became one of life and death for the large trout.

I waited a week before going after him again, hoping that he would stay where he was as the midsummer waters receded. As the weather returned to the usual heat of mid-July, I opted to go after him in the cool of the morning.

It was about 8:00 a.m. on the day I chose to do battle, and I had to wait only a moment or two after my arrival at his lair for him to appear. I eagerly began to wade into a sensible casting position, but in the reduced flow I sent telltale waves over the trout, which then refused to feed. I stood in midstream for a half-hour, hoping that he would resume feeding, but he did not; so I left and dealt with other trout which were in more easily approached positions.

By this time I was really obsessed with the demise of this trout. I dreamed of him nightly, and I attempted to catch him two or three times each week for the next month, but to no avail. He rose faithfully each day that I visited the meadow, but long casts would not float over him, though once he did swirl at a luckily cast ant. I was unable to find a proper way to approach him without scaring him, and it appeared that he was safe, at least from me.

One afternoon in early August, I showed Bruce the lair of the perplexing fish. When he saw the fish's location on the left bank (facing upstream), Bruce, who is a southpaw, asked whether there were any trout in the riffle upstream from the trout's feeding station.

Small fries," I answered. "Why?"

"Well, Rich," he replied, "I can cross the creek there and walk down the other bank. Then I can cast and float my fly under the tree by giving line and letting the current carry my fly to the trout. If I'm lucky, he'll take an ant."

I agreed that he could employ this sensible tactic, for as a lefty he could extend his rod tip out over the bank more easily than I could, enabling him to cast from above the trout. By doing this, he would successfully avoid becoming entangled in the high weeds on the bank behind him. Meanwhile, I sat on the bank across from the tree to observe his progress. The cast and float of his fly were perfect. When the ant arrived at the trout's feeding station, the trout gently inhaled it.

"Pull!" I screamed like a teenage cheerleader at a basketball game, but Bruce struck a little late and merely scratched the trout. A minute later he was back with me and explained that one of the fronds of grass, which had grown considerably since May, had obstructed his view, and he hadn't seen the trout's actual rise, only its rise form. The trout had dodged yet another bullet, though Bruce suggested that I could use his tactic. Instead of casting, though, I would coil my line in the water at the edge of the creek, gently shake it through my rod guides, and allow the current to float it and my fly toward the fish. This seemed to be a perfect solution to my dilemma of how best to approach the trout, and I used this method the next several times I was after him.

However, despite his continued attraction to floating foods, he would not be deceived by any of my artifices. I tried caddisses, imitation beetles, crickets, and a variety of tiny bits of feathers and fur on size 22 and 24 hooks, such as jassids and midget ants, but nothing worked. By mid-August I was spending most of my fishing time elsewhere, with more easily deceived trout, including several dandy wild browns which were bigger than any of the other fish I had caught all season. Despite the successes, the trout at the walnut tree continued to haunt me.

On the evening of Aug. 17, during the "dog days" of late summer, my wife and son were visiting some neighbors, and I decided to make my first evening venture to the meadow since early in June. I harbored little hope of catching my elusive opponent; the water was low, warm, and ultra-clear, and I did not expect to find him rising.

When I arrived at the walnut tree, I sloppily sent out a cast before I had even bothered to watch for my trout. The toss was rewarded with

Bruce Houck helped the author capture the elusive trout at the walnut tree. As a left-handed fisherman, Houck was able to extend his rod tip over the bank more easily than Tate could, enabling Houck to cast from above the trout.

a splashy rise, which turned out to be a small fallfish, and its presence and disruption of the pool put my thought of the big trout to rest. Heck, I wasn't even discouraged: The cumulative effects of my previous failures had made this fallfish affair, if not expected, at least bearable.

I contentedly departed the lair of the educated trout and went below the little dam to fish. At dusk a few whitish mayflies began to hatch, much to my surprise. I quickly caught and released several colorful wild brown trout with bright yellow bellies and deep red spots splattered gaily along their grayish flanks. When I approached the flat water home of my adversary, I found him there, feeding actively, although this time he had erred. He had moved a couple of feet upstream, above the grassy overhang, enabling me to wade into the creek a short distance, allowing a proper presentation of my fly.

I had knotted on a size 14 Cream Variant at the onset of the sparse hatch, and after several unrewarded casts in the near dark, I believed that the fish was going to survive yet another test in this life-and-death contest.

But my sixth cast went slightly awry, and my fly dragged perceptibly enough for me to note it scratching the surface of the mirror-like pool. The trout must have sensed that the movement indicated life and struck savagely. My reaction was just that, an unthinking reaction. I drove the point of the hook into the trout's mouth. His reaction was also immediate. He plowed downstream, passed the roots of the tree, and zoomed toward the dam. I stumbled along the bank after him, hoping to get below him to force a fight upstream, which would tire him. My plan succeeded, as the fish tried several times to run upstream against the gentle but opposing flow of the current. The trout was also without the heavier volume of water he had enjoyed on our previous hookup, and I was able to establish firm control of the battle in only a couple of minutes.

Even with a light tippet, I was able to force him toward the mud beach where I had laid my landing net. For the next several minutes the fish circled as his strength waned, and finally I was able to guide him into the net. When his head and shoulders were lying over the mesh, I grabbed the handle and lifted, and he was subdued. It had not been an epic battle; the entire fight had lasted no more than seven or eight minutes, probably less. Even so, I was trembling when I saw that even though the trout was doubled in the mesh, his tail extended out over the net's frame.

I had thoughts of releasing the 20-inch, hook-jawed, male brown which had certainly challenged my fishing skills, but I quickly dispatched him, not wanting him to suffer needlessly when I made my final decision to kill him.

Upon arriving at home, I noisily burst into the house and yelled for my wife to come to the kitchen. Donna knew from my excitement that I had finally caught the trout I had been after all summer, and she listened patiently as I repeated my tale several times, slightly embellishing the actual battle. I am sure she expected that of me.

Even though my stated reason for killing the trout had been to have him mounted, it never happened. Living on one income at the time and having plenty of bills to pay, the extravagance of having the fish stuffed to satisfy my vanity was something that was not justifiable. Instead, Donna baked the large trout, which provided the centerpiece for a large family dinner.

Do I harbor regrets about killing the large trout? Sure I do. I recognize that few trout in my home waters ever attain the size that this fine trout did, that he was more exciting as a fishing adversary than he was after I had slain him.

However, at the time, my human instincts as a predator won out, and I made what is almost a ritualistic kill that reminded me of that fact. Although I have caught and released several larger trout in the years since our encounter, the trout at the walnut tree remains the most memorable large trout I have landed to this time.

Chapter 8

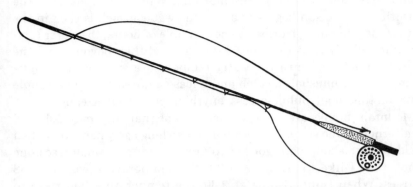

FAVORITE FISHING STRATEGIES:
(1) Fishing the Water

In the area of central Pennsylvania where I live, a good 70-75 percent of the trout season from mid-April through the end of October is spent fishing during the absense of fly hatches. Because of this, I have had to develop a set of tactics to use when aquatic flies are not arousing the feeding urges of the trout. I don't think anything I've discovered is new or revolutionary. However, I have sifted through thousands of pages of fly-fishing writing and have spent thousands of hours astream, and what I am about to tell you works well for me.

"Fishing the water" means casting your flies to locations in creeks and rivers where you think trout will be lurking. Areas favorable for fishing the water include deep pockets along tangles of tree roots, areas along submerged logs, sections of stream along undercut banks, water near in-stream structures such as submerged rocks, and stream sections where riffles spill into pools. Over the years, I have found these types of places to be the most productive when I am out prospecting for trout.

I have also recognized the importance of water temperatures in governing trout activity. The brown trout's optimum temperature is about 62 or 63 degrees, depending upon which studies you read, and the brook trout's is a couple of degrees lower. As a creek's temperature approaches the optimum, the more active the trout seem to be. Leonard Wright's *The Ways of Trout* discusses why he thinks this is true: I only know that it really is true on the streams I frequent.

For example, the Little Shawnee fishes well for me in midsummer from about 9:00 to 11:00 in the morning. Why? At about 9:00, the warmth from the sun begins to affect the water, which is then in the 58 to 60 degree range. During the next couple of hours, the water temperature quickly rises to 63 or 64 degrees and then beyond, and the trout feed actively until the water temperature exceeds their optimum. It is not unusual to catch and release a dozen trout in a couple hours on this small, public-access, anything-goes trout stream.

Mountain brooks are quite similar, except that they may fish well all afternoon. One summer afternoon not so long ago when Donna had decided to go shopping, I got her to drop me off at a small freestone brook that I like to fish. At 11:00, the temperature was only 58 degrees. When I quit fishing at 2:30, the temperature had risen to almost 62 degrees. How did I do? How does 50 wild brown and brook trout strike you? These sparkling jewels, all between six and 13 inches, greedily attacked my Wright Caddis for several hours and would probably have continued to do so until the water temperature rose above 66 or 67 degrees. I should have caught many more trout than I did: I missed at least half the trout that attacked my fraud.

My fishing notebooks are filled with many similar episodes, and though I do not take the temperature of the water every time I am astream because I have learned to recognize when my favorite streams will fish well through experience, I am well aware of the importance of water temperature's effect on trout activity.

My fishing notebooks also include some horrid examples of days I experienced poor fishing because I did not pay attention to the temperature of the water until it was too late. One recent episode occurred on a damp, drizzly April day on a little mountain stream. I didn't bother to take the water temperature when I began to fish that day. I just "knew" that the hungry trout in this stream would greedily attack the little Grizzly Parachute I like to use there. Bad move.

In two hours of fishing I landed only a half-dozen junior leaguers. I did check the water temperature before I left: 52 degrees. It had probably been within a degree or two of that the entire time I was there, never moving toward the optimum, contributing to the cause of the lacklustre afternoon of fishing. Negative experiences such as this have reinforced my contention that water temperature is probably the most important element of fly-fishing when you are fishing the water.

High water temperatures also negatively influence fishing. If a trout stream heats up to about 70 degrees and stays there for very long, the trout become pretty sluggish, and many head for the oxygenated water of the riffles or lie torpidly in the bottoms of deep pools. Five degrees more, and the trout will probably migrate to spring holes or to the upper reaches of the stream where the temperature is more to their liking. Being aware of this can help you to avoid too many fishless days on streams where what amounts to thermal pollution exists. Finding the spring holes can lead you to some exciting fishing, especially on marginal waters.

When you are fishing the water, especially in midsummer on small, clear streams, it is best to be as unobtrusive as you can. This means that you should wade only when necessary so that you won't send out shock waves that will frighten the trout. It also means that you ought to dress in subdued colors to help mask your movements. I generally wear old, green work shirts; my old, stained fishing vest; and a camouflage cap to try to blend into the streamside background. Unless I am fishing with wet flies, I slowly fish my way upstream to try to avoid having the trout spot me. I really believe that paying attention to these seemingly minor details at least doubles the number of trout I get into during an outing.

You've got to find some effective flies to successfully fish the water, too. I've settled on two dry flies for the bulk of my summer probing: the Wright Caddis and a little Grizzly Parachute. Here are their patterns:

WRIGHT CADDIS
Hook — size 14, 16 Mustad 94840
Thread — black
Tail — none
Body — peacock herl, wound with fine gold tinsel
Hackle — ginger or dun rooster hackle feather
Wing — ginger or dun feather fibers, laid back of hackle over the body

GRIZZLY PARACHUTE
Hook — size 14, 16 Mustad 94840
Thread — black
Tail — grizzly feather fibers
Body — muskrat fur
Hackle — grizzly, wound parachute style
Wing — white calf tail
Both of these fly patterns take trout consistently for me.

You might wonder about the wisdom of fishing dry flies instead of underwater flies when fishing the water. The assertion that 85-90 percent of a trout's food is underwater has been popularized over many years. Maybe it's true, too. However, I do 85-90 percent of my fishing on creeks that a good broad jumper could leap across in many places. They don't contain holes more than three or three-and-a-half feet

One of the author's favorite flies is a Wright Fluttering Caddis, which he uses to successfully "fish the water."

A Grizzly Parachute is a good fly to use in wooded areas, according to fly-fishing experts. This is also a good fly to use to "fish the water."

deep in most places, and their trout are on the lookout for food items on the surface as well as under the surface, even in the absense of hatches. These opportunistic trout will eagerly pounce on a decently presented dry fly under normal water conditions.

I like to drift my flies near cover and along in-stream structures where the trout feel safe. Let's face facts: Most trout that do not take advantage of structure and that feed out in the open are quickly caught and creeled on most hard-fished, public-access trout streams. The survivors are the ones that make use of the stream's safety features.

I like the Wright Caddis for probing relatively open sections of stream. It is a good floater and is easy to see under most conditions. Though the trout take it readily, I don't think they always take it for a caddis. Its silhouette resembles that of a lot of bugs, including small grasshoppers and houseflies. Whatever the reasons, the Wright Caddis is a super fish finder.

On deeply shaded freestone brooks, I have gone to the Grizzly Parachute. Introduced to the fly by Ray Neirle one steamy July day when I was leading the then 81-year-old enthusiast on a mile hike along a mountain brook, I have found the little parachute to be a wonderful trout taker. In addition, it is very easy to see in shaded areas of streams.

The season Ray showed me the fly will help illustrate how well it works. The evening after the trip Ray and I shared, I whipped up a half-dozen of the little flies, and the next day I visited a different section of the creek Ray and I had fished the previous day. In less than three hours, I had landed 15 brown and rainbow trout up to 14 inches from the heavily fished brook. I continued to fish that brook with the Grizzly Parachute the rest of the summer, and eight is the fewest number of trout I caught during any outing. The Grizzly Parachute now occupies an important compartment of my dry fly box and is a fly I confidently tie on when I am fishing on small freestone creeks.

Don't I ever fish underwater? Yes, but I prefer floaters. However, when the water in the small creeks is higher than normal from rains, or when I'm fishing on larger rivers, I'll knot on a duo of nymphs or wet flies. The wet flies I prefer are the standard patterns of the Leadwing Coachman and the thread-bodied Black Ant, in sizes 10 and 12. When I'm using wet flies, I edge my way downstream, casting across or slightly upstream, allowing the flies to sink, then drift them through the stream's pockets and pools, finally allowing the flies to swing back to my side of the creek. I have landed a fair number of 15-inch and larger trout on these flies and probably ought to use them more often than I do.

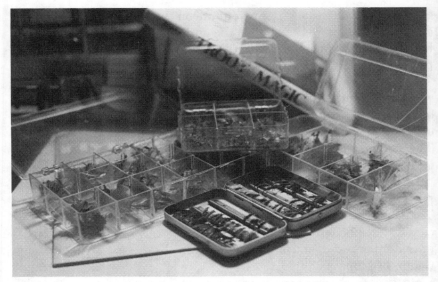

Sometimes a fly-fisherman faces the dilemma of which fly to use, especially when he has an assortment of flies, as shown here.

Big waters without obviously feeding trout pose a different challenge. On these rivers, you need weighted flies, and you'll probably need to work harder to catch trout than you do on small waters. The over-publicized Little Juniata River is one such stream near my home. When I fish the Little Juniata in the absense of surface activity, I employ a brace of weighted nymphs, often a large Stonefly (size 8) and often a little black nymph in size 10 or 12. I weight the heck out of these so that they will go to the bottom. On this large stream (by Eastern standards), I drift the nymphs through rapidly moving water at the base of rapids and through pockets of relatively calm water in riffle areas. Often I need to add one or two size B split shot to help sink the already heavily weighted flies. At one time I fished these on a sink-tip fly line, but I've gone back to fishing them on a nine-foot leader attached to a floating line. I think I detect more strikes with the floating line than I did when I favored the sink-tip line. Fluorescent orange strike indicators are extremely helpful when nymphing, too. However, I am one who wrestles with the concern whether the use of strike indicators is legitimate fly-fishing, especially the ones that act as bobbers. That they increase your hook-ups is undeniable: The slightest movement of the indicator usually means *fish,* and you set the hook. However, the ones that float high in the water certainly act as bobbers and really suspend the flies below them. It is inelegant and could easily be performed with spinning or spincast gear. It certainly decreases the skill level needed for success. Anyhow, I have only begun to use the strike indicators for my stream probing, and I am not sure they entirely belong to the world of fly-fishing. As other anglers have observed, they may provide an unfair advantage for the nymph fisherman.

Do nymphs work? They sure do. Expert nymph fishermen tell tales of regularly landing two-dozen trout on nymphs. For me on the Little Juniata, landing 10 or 12 trout is a good day. On smaller creeks, using a pair of Hare's Ear nymphs, 12 to 15 trout in a couple hours is a good outing for me when I'm fishing the water with nymphs.

I've also found that nymph fishing success occurs in spurts, unlike dry fly fishing to the water where the hook-ups seem to occur on a more even basis. One of my first good days with the nymphs occurred on a cool July afternoon a couple years ago. I was using the Hare's Ear nymphs on the small branch of the Little Shawnee.

For the first hour I had only an occasional bump, and I was about ready to call it quits. At about 3:15, it was as though a dinner bell had sounded, and the trout went nuts. Although there was no hatch of flies and no surface feeding, every pocket or riffle into which I pitched the little nymphs erupted with strikes from frenzied trout. I landed 15 trout and lost several others by 4:15, when the creek suddenly went dead. Experienced nymph fishermen tell me that this is a common occurrence. They say that biologists attribute these spurts to the regular mass movement of nymphs as they redistribute themselves in a stream. Many of the dislodged nymphs float a distance before reattaching themselves to their new homes, and the trout attack them during this vulnerable time. Biologists call this *drift*. It is a neat-sounding explanation, maybe too neat, but it does help to explain sudden explosions of feeding by the trout on subsurface flies.

Sometimes I'll probe a particularly good-looking pool with a black Wooly Bugger when I'm out prospecting. I often place a size B split shot right at the head of the fly to sink it, though I usually drift it as I would a brace of wet flies. On occasion, the Wooly Bugger will account for fine trout that I otherwise would not have caught.

The size of the trout you catch when prospecting will vary from stream to stream. Using dry flies on small creeks, I expect the trout to average seven to 12 inches, a size I expect to duplicate with nymphs on these waters. On larger rivers, I expect the trout to run a little larger, though in recent seasons the average size of the trout I get a hold of on the Little Juniata has sadly decresed. For a time, I thought it was just me, but Little Juniata regulars are bewailing this in print now.

A Black Ant wet fly can come in handy. The author prefers a wet fly when fishing in larger rivers or swollen streams.

You can get into some rip-snorters when fishing the water, too. I've caught trout of 20 inches while fishing wet flies, and they can give you a real jolt. One July morning I was fishing the Leadwing Coachman and Black Ant tandem on the Little Shawnee but wasn't doing beans. I was ready to head elsewhere on this steamy July morning. Luckily, I didn't. In a place where the creek swings under the branches of a small willow, I felt a slight tug, and I set the hook. That hook-up began a 15-minute tussle with a heavy brown trout that taped at slightly under 21 inches. He bulldogged along the bottom, never making any furious runs. It was not the type of battle that can be described as epic or exciting. Rather, it was nerve-wracking for me and would've been boring to watch as I maneuvered my rod in various ways to make the trout tire himself. Fortunately for me, the ugly, hook-jawed male wore out before my wrist did.

I have caught fish of 18 inches from the Little Shawnee when using dry flies to fish the water. I recently snaked one out from underneath a cut bank. I thought he was surely 20 inches when I hooked him. However, when I had him in my net, he had shrunk a couple inches under my estimation, which is still a pretty fine trout. I was pleased to catch him. The most unusual thing about this trout was the time of day I caught him: 12:30 p.m. I'm usually done fishing by that time and am ready to head for the old swimming pool, but this morning was unusually cool, and the trout didn't become active till nearly 11:30 a.m., which kept me on the creek much longer than usual. The big trout would probably have ignored my fly an hour earlier. If I had used my water thermometer that morning I probably would have known that the best fishing was not going to occur until it did.

Anyhow, fishing to the water can extend your fishing season by 70-75 percent in many areas. I have found that though it doesn't usually produce the concentrated bursts of activity that mayfly hatches produce, it can provide steadier action when the water is right. If you like to catch trout, don't be afraid to do a little prospecting on the trout streams in your area: They may very pleasantly surprise you.

Chapter 9

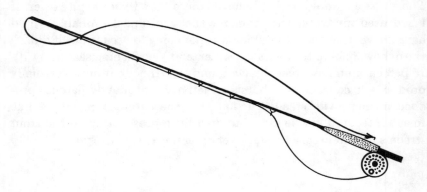

AFTER DARK

The cover of darkness means many things to many people. For criminals, it provides a cloak for their nefarious activities. For lovers, starlit nights provide romantic, quiet settings for their trysts. For most people it is a time for an hour or two of TV then off to bed. For trout fishermen, it ends their days astream. Well, mostly.

There are a few crazed souls in the world of fishing who continue to fish after darkness descends. Most are bait fishermen who specialize in catching lunker trout. A few are fly-fishermen. The best-known of the after-dark fly-fishers is Joe Humphreys, former Professor of Angling at Penn State University whose night-caught 16-pound brown trout held the Pennsylvania state record for a number of years.

In my bailiwick, Pike DiBartolome was the best-known night fisherman. He used live baits such as grasshoppers to send many large trout to their doom.

"Why don't you try it?" he asked me several times during my early years astream. "That's when you catch big trout."

"How big?"

"I have gotten a lot of 18-to 20-inch trout after dark over the years. Those are about as big as trout normally get on the Little Shawnee."

"Do you think they would take flies?"

"I don't see why not," he smiled as he chewed the stump of a cigar. "Just tie some bigger than the ones you use during the day. A lot of the big trout I catch after dark take my bait or 'hopper just as it hits the water."

"I don't know. It's pretty dangerous out there at night. You don't know who or what is out there," I replied. I worry about dogs and druggies when I fish, though my conversations with Pike occurred in the days before drug use really skyrocketed.

"Who's around?" Pike chuckled. "No one's around the creek after dark. The biggest scare I ever had was from a couple of farmers who thought I was cattle rustling one night. Otherwise, a noisy raccoon or a nosy skunk is all the closer I've ever been to danger."

DiBartolome's exploits were legendary in my hometown, but despite his urgings, I was satisified to fish during the day for a good many years. Night fishing was for the crazies.

Finally, though, I enlisted in the ranks of the crazies. I was fishing my trusty Wright Caddis along a meadow stretch of the Little Shawnee one steamy July evening, and when I reached the upper end of the meadow, I was fishless. I hate to get skunked. No matter what the poets and philosophers say about the beauty of nature being a key element of fishing, I'm not happy with fishless outings. Oh, sure, I like a nice, sunny day along the creek as well as the next guy, but I'd rather catch fish in the rain than be skunked in the sunshine.

At any rate, I was trying to figure out what to do.

Why don't you use wet flies and fish back down to the Scout? I asked myself. You don't have anything to lose. Heck, you might even catch a trout.

I rigged up a brace of wet flies and started back down the creek. Bang! On my first cast I was into a trout, and after a brief but spirited struggle, I had the chunky 12-incher beside me, ready to release. A couple casts later, and bang! again. Another fiesty trout tested my little fiberglass rod before I could beach him. What was going on here?

It was really dark by now, but I had another hundred yards to go to the Scout, and I wasn't quitting yet. Good thing: It wasn't too long before the next trout hit, and when I set the hook, there was no give from the other end.

I think other writers have used all the adjectives that describe battles such as the one in which I became engaged for the next several minutes. The big trout tore down the creek, with me in hot pursuit. He easily negotiated a riffle under a barbed wire fence that gave me a lot of trouble. I probably would've looked pretty ridiculous to the lightning bugs if they could have realized what the creature was that was pulling himself loose from the barbed wire fence. Finally, though, the trout settled down to slug it out in a long, flat pool. But his long run had tired him, and within minutes I was able to beach him. He was a little longer than the 18-inch landing net I carried at the time, a real lunker on the Little Shawnee. I was one very smug trout fisherman when I got home and related my tale of triumph to Donna. She was not impressed, saying something about fathers who aren't around at their children's bedtime.

That evening was the unintended beginning of my after-dark quests for trout. Before I went fishing after dark again, I re-read the book about the dark art that had lain on a shelf of my fly tying room for nearly 10 years. I tied a couple of big wet flies that the author recommended, and I figured I was ready to purposefully pursue trout under the cover of darkness.

Over the next few years, a few wet flies emerged as my favorites. I liked to use the Black Ant and Leadwing Coachman in size 10 on the Little Shawnee, and on larger waters like the Little Juniata River, I developed a preference for size 6 and 8 Governors and later for size 6 and 8 Wooly Buggers. According to what I've read, however, these are considered to be small flies for night fishing. Despite this, they do a good job of catching trout for me.

I even talked Bruce into going with me one summer night. "There are a few flies hatching before dark," I told him. Bruce, a real dry fly purist, agreed to go along only after I'd told him about the hatching mayflies.

It turned out to be the best night of after-dark trout fishing I had enjoyed to that date and still ranks as one of my best. I watched Bruce fish to the few risers before I plodded in above him, and he landed a couple average Little Juniata browns before I began to fish. I made my first cast when I could still see my hand in front of my face, and the cast was rewarded with a solid take. A minute or two later, I skidded the 12-inch brown to my hand and shook him off my Governor. As the darkness increased, so did the action. In the next half-hour or so, I picked up four more average river browns of 10 to 12 inches and a rare (for the Little Juniata) 15-inch rainbow. I totally forgot that Bruce was even around. The next trout was a reel-sceecher that battled noisily in the dark.

"Is that another trout?" Bruce called.

"Yep. He feels like the best one so far," and when I beached him, Bruce taped him at slightly under 18 inches. "Do you want to try now?" I asked.

"No, you go ahead," Bruce replied, and I was happy to continue to fish — and to catch trout.

After a couple more junior leaguers, I hit another dandy. Again I fought the battle by feel and by sound in the darkness. It was quite awhile before I beached this one, a sleek 19-inch brown that we measured by the light of Bruce's little penlight.

"Are you ready to try it yet?" I asked Bruce, and this time he agreed to fish. There was a curious edge to his voice as he replied.

A couple of minutes after he waded in, I heard the whine from Bruce's reel as it surrendered the line to what sounded like a big trout. I sat admiring the sounds of the fierce struggle, and I knelt beside Bruce when he beached the large trout. This fish turned out to be the fish of the night, a 20-inch brown, the largest I had ever seen on the overfished Little Juniata.

"What fly did you use?" I asked. Bruce doesn't even carry wet flies a lot of the time.

"A big, yellow Wooly Worm. My gosh, Rich, this was incredible. Trout really do go nuts after dark, don't they?"

I agreed that they do — sometimes. I have suffered a good many blank nights on the stream, too, and I believe that trout are moodier after dark than they are during the day.

"The darker the night, the better," Pike and others used to say, and to a certain degree, that seems to be true. I have enjoyed my best fishing on nights that there was no moon but plenty of stars. I've not had much success on either moonlit nights or cloudy nights, and in the interest of marital harmony, I am no longer on the stream on those types of nights. Curiously, arc lights near farms on the Little Shawnee don't seem to bother the trout, though. I've caught a fair number of nice trout during the past several years from pools only 50-60 yards from bright arc lights. I can't figure out why the trout there are so receptive when the trout are so tough under bright moonlight, but I don't argue with success.

I had pretty much gotten over my initial concerns about fishing after dark until a couple of incidents in the mid-1980s again put me on edge. The first incident occurred one night on a backroad stretch of the Little Shawnee. I had parked the little pickup I bought to replace my old, trusty, rusty Scout where I thought passers-by wouldn't notice it, and I sallied forth to do battle. I fished for a couple hours, but I did not catch any noteworthy trout. Figuring it was time to head for home, I climbed the bank to the path leading to the truck. I heard voices. I halted and listened for a few minutes. When I heard both male and female voices, I decided to walk directly past what I figured were a few teenagers. It wasn't real smart: It turned out that I strode rather brazenly past a six- or seven-car party, and there were 18 or 20 young women and men of a variety of ages up to 30 or so.

The other incident occurred on a remote section of the Little Juniata River. I had been fishing for an hour or so when I saw car lights cross the bridge below me where I had parked. The car lights went out, only yards from my little pickup, I thought. I again figured it was a couple of teenagers, and I didn't worry too much about it and continued to fish for the next hour or more. The trout didn't cooperate, and when I walked back down the river to my truck, I could see that the car was still there, too. When I approached my truck, I noticed two guys sitting on the hood of their car, hoisting cans of what I assumed was beer. Trying to act nonchalant as I passed them, I asked them if they had an extra beer.

"No, these are the last ones we have," one replied gruffly, as I obviously startled him. He didn't sound like a teenage kid, either.

I kept going, and the other one said, "That's a good way to get shot," and added something else I didn't quite catch.

I hastily got into my truck without taking off my waders or vest, and I quickly got out of there. If the two drunks had a gun, I figured I could be in deep trouble.

I was pretty shaky when I got home that night, and Donna agreed that a pistol might be a sound investment in my future if I continued to encounter late-evening situations like these. I haven't yet obtained a handgun. However, every time I've seen car lights when I'm night fishing during the past couple seasons, I get a little nervous until they have passed.

I've also considered abandoning the dark art, but there are too many times that the local lunkers are active for me to chicken out. Only a couple of weeks after my encounter with the pair of beer drinkers, I landed a 19-inch brown from a pool near when they'd frightened me.

I've also enjoyed some dandy outings on the Little Shawnee since my close encounter with the group of party-goers. The best of these was much like the one that Bruce and I tore them up on the Little Juniata.

Besides being a good time to catch larger than average trout, night fishing is usually a time for solitude when on the stream. Many trout waters are pounded to a froth by diurnal anglers, but these same streams are deserted after nightfall. A solitary angler can fish all the water he wants without having to worry about interference from the maddening crowd. He can drift into reverie as his line swishes, cutting through the darkness. The sounds of the night — crickets, katydids, owls — provide a soothing balm for the wounds caused by our frenetic, over-civilized world.

No, night fishing is not a game for everyone. A careless step could cause a serious injury or even death on a large river, and encounters with midnight riders are a real possibility.

Even so, I think the positives far outweigh the negatives, and I will continue to reserve eight to 10 nights each summer to practice the dark art. Though it's a much different game from daylight fly-fishing, it is a form of fly-fishing that casts an enchantment over those of us who are drawn to it.

A black Wooly Bugger is a dandy night fly, often used by the author when he's "out prospecting" for trout after the sun sets.

Chapter 10

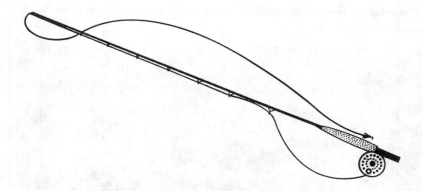

ANGLER'S BULLFIGHT

During midsummer, I like to fish meadow sections of the Little Shawnee Creek. The trusty Wright Caddis is an effective fly in these areas, and the flycasting is easy. Often these meadows are used as pastures by area farmers, and their grazing animals keep the nasty weeds and bushes trimmed effectively.

Not too many years ago, I had driven out to fish one of the lovely meadow sections of the small branch of the Little Shawnee. The farm that this meadow belonged to had recently changed hands, and I was thankful that the new owner had not erected "no trespassing" signs.

I particularly liked fishing in this meadow. The stream is quite small here — maybe 15 feet across — but boasts a fair number of nice pools. In addition, it is one of the few places on the Little Shawnee that trout will rise to *Tricorythodes* mayflies. As difficult as it is to believe, the trout ignore Tricos on most sections of the little creek, preferring larger mouthfuls of food.

It was a lovely summer morning. Even I admired the diamond-like sparkling of the dew on the green summer grasses. There was a slight chill to the air, a chill that would soon dissipate under the hot summer sun. After parking, I walked about a half mile down the creek before starting to fish. At one point, I crawled under a two-strand barbed wire fence, being careful not to tear a hole in my hip boots. Barbed wire has cost me more than one pair of good hippers.

As I rigged up, I noticed a couple of Holsteins grazing behind me under an old apple tree. "Good," I smiled, aloud, "only two cows. Maybe they won't even bother me today."

I have often encountered small herds of cows on my fishing adventures. The previous landowner had often pastured groups of heifers in this meadow, and their bovine curiosity had sometimes sent them my way as they tried to figure out what the crazy guy waving the funny stick and string was doing. Occasionally, one or two would even nuzzle me as I knelt to cast. Though kind of irritating at times, I had always figured it was a small price to pay for free access to the fishing in the meadow.

I had no more than made my first cast into the pool where I'd chosen to begin my fishing when I heard a deep slurp in the swampy ground behind me. Startled, I jumped to my feet from a kneeling position. One of the Holsteins, knee-deep in muck, was glaring at me, angrily shaking his huge head back and forth, looking much like a gigantic whitetail buck battling a tree during the rutting season.

Oh my Lord, it's a bull, I gulped as I looked at him, and he's all fired up.

Lest someone think I overreacted here, let me say that I have no fear of most animals. While fishing, I have run into bears, poisonous snakes, and other so-called beasts, and most of them have been much more afraid of me than I was of them. In fact, one bear that I met along a little mountain brook got a whiff of me at 60 or 70 yards, and in his haste to get away from me, scrambled up a steep bank that I thought couldn't be scaled by man or beast.

Only an occasional German shepherd or Doberman puts the fear of God into me when I'm fishing.

In addition, my father-in-law and brother-in-law operate a beef farm, and I have helped them round up their cattle on occasion. However, living in farm country, I also recognize the danger that bulls can pose toward humans. Every year or two, it seems, I read of a farm worker being attacked by a bull. In addition, one of my friends once told me that in the days before artificial insemination, bulls were the number one source of danger on farms.

I was scared hollow in the bowels, and if I hadn't relieved myself before starting to fish, the bull could have trailed me out of the meadow. For no apparent reason, this bull was enraged, and as he tore at the ground to free himself from the muck, he snorted angrily through flared nostrils, continuing to toss his head wildly about.

Holy cow, I punned fearfully to myself, I can see it now. Tomorrow's newspaper is going to read "Local Angler Killed by Mad Bull" unless I can figure a way out of this mess — and fast.

Deciding to bluff the huge animal, I ran at him, screaming like a banshee, but he retreated only a step or two and savagely began to paw the drier ground. I knew my ruse had failed, that I had a 2,000-pound animal ready to rip me apart with his horns and then trample me under his murderous hooves. It would be a very unpleasant way to die.

I was a couple hundred yards downstream from the fence I'd crawled under to enter the meadow — and safety. I sure couldn't out-run the bull to the fence. So, I gradually backed into the tail of the pool and through it, opting to use the big willow on the other side of the creek and the deep pool for protection. The bull glared nastily at me through bloodshot eyes as I made the crossing, but I managed to reach the shelter of the willow without being charged. As the bull bellowed and snorted angrily, I looked at the tree trunk I had hoped to climb: There was not even one substantial limb within nine or ten feet of the ground. Terrified, I knew that the tree was not going to provide the sanctuary I needed.

How was I going to escape? I recalled a Dana Lamb tale in which a night fisherman had escaped from an enraged bull by taking a small boat to safety. But I had no boat. I had to try to deal with this raging bull intent on slaughter.

I finally realized I was at the downstream tip of a narrow strip of trees that extended upstream, to within 60 or 70 yards of the barbed wire fence. If only I could get to that fence!

My entire body was soaked with sweat — and not from the heat of the sun — as I slowly stepped from behind the sentinel willow and cautiously eased my way 10 feet to the next protective tree.

As I agonizingly crept from tree to tree, the bull easily kept pace by trotting along the opposite bank, constantly snorting and shaking his head — but not crossing the little creek. It took me a long time to reach the upstream end of the line of protective trees. At about the same time as I arrived there, the bull was joined by another huge Holstein, a large steer. I irrationally decided that they were plotting to team up on me.

I also knew it was "do or die" time. Eventually the two animals would cross the creek, gore me, and then stomp me into mush. I sure couldn't take off my vest and use it as a matador's cape. My fiberglass rod would be equally useless as a lance. The only emotion I could feel was a chilling fear, as I decided that I had to reach the safety of the other side of the fence.

After I had made the decision to head for the fence, I knelt and picked up a volleyball-sized rock. Screaming epithets quite unprintable, I heaved the rock into the creek at the bull's feet.

Encumbered in hip boots and a heavy fishing vest that Bruce tells me weighs about three times more than his, I immediately began to sprint for the fence, amazed that the bull had hesitantly retreated from my screaming and rock toss.

However, it didn't take the bull long to regain his anger, and I heard him and his cohort begin to gallop after me. I felt slight spasms of relief as I passed several small pools the bull would have trouble negotiating. My heart was pounding in my ears, my lungs were ready to explode, and my legs felt like collapsing rubber bands as I desperately raced for the fence.

When I was only 15 feet from sanctuary, I heard the two beasts blast across a shallow riffle only a few yards behind me, and I strained in terror for the fence. Five feet from safety, I heaved my rod toward some shrubs above the barbed wire. The beasts were pounding right behind me. A step later I groped for a metal fence post and vaulted over the strands of barbed wire.

As I crashed headlong into some streamside mint and mud, I wondered whether the thin strands of wire would actually halt the murderous bull and the steer. I hid my head under my arms.

Several minutes passed, and I realized that I had indeed survived. My nemesis and his companion were prancing around the meadow in triumph as I got up and wiped the muck from my clothes and face and as I washed the blood from my hands which had skidded on some stones when I landed. I was a mess, but I was alive.

I was shaking uncontrollably when I picked up my rod and left what had been one of my favorite Little Shawnee meadows. The raging bull kept its trout off limits to me for several years, until the owner finally quit pasturing him there.

Chapter 11

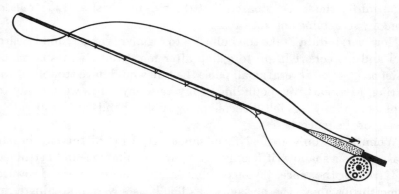

FAVORITE FISHING STRATEGIES: (2) Fishing During Mayfly Hatches

During my formative years as a flyrodder, when I began to explore some of the vast literature of the sport, I began to encounter many treatises about fishing during hatches of mayflies. As a newcomer to the sport, I found a lot of this material confusing and not a bit helpful. The terminology was not explained well in many cases. What in heaven's name was a *dun*? What kind of fly was a *spinner*? The only kind of spinner I'd ever heard of was one that had a flashy metal blade and was cranked through the water by spin fishermen.

Of course, the books of Flick, Marinaro, and Schweibert finally rescued me from the abyss of ignorance, and soon I began to recognize that there were three distinct stages of a mayfly hatch: nymphs, duns, and spinners. Each could be imitated by the fly-fisherman to effectively deal with feeding trout.

Over the years, I have discovered that fly-fishermen actually can catch trout at four different levels during a mayfly hatch. The first level is down deep, the level at which I personally catch very few fish, especially during mayfly hatches. I just don't like to fish down deep when I know that trout will be surface feeding, though I know it can be effective. Fishing with weighted nymphs of a species of fly that will be hatching can be done all day in anticipation of the actual hatch, and to me, that is just like fishing to the water with nymphs. My preference is to let that for the nymph fishing addicts who'll often con-

White water areas provide good oxygenation, keeping streams healthy for trout and other wildlife. (Photo courtesy Paul Tofte)

tinue to fish underwater even in the presence of surface-feeding trout! I don't know how they can do that, but they do. One such fellow, I'm told, even sold his entire collection of Metz dry fly capes for $10 per neck. Had I known, I'd have bought the whole bunch.

For me, fishing to a mayfly hatch begins when the flies actually begin to show on the surface. This is the emergence — the hatch. I've found that it is necessary to carry a couple fly styles to use during the actual emergence of mayflies. One is called an emerger — a fly that imitates a nymph which is ascending or that has ascended to the surface of the stream before it transforms into a winged sub-adult fly called a dun. These emergers can be fished several inches underwater to trout that are feeding just below the surface, or they can be floated in the surface film if the trout are taking the emerging naturals there. I once heard a noted fly-fisherman say that these latter flies are properly called floating nymphs, and he was right, of course. I've found that I can fish the emergers I tie at both levels. The emergers I tie to imitate most hatches will float, since I tie them on dry fly hooks, but if the trout want them a little deeper, I soak them with saliva in my mouth. They'll sink then. I know that that's a heck of a thing to do with a fly, but if you want to catch trout, you've got to put the fly where the fish want it.

The emergers I use are really easy to tie. I tie the tail and hackle collar with feathers of the same color as the legs of the naturals, dub a body that corresponds to that of the real fly's, and tie in a wing case I make from rolled nylon from discarded pantyhose. I make this wing case extend about halfway back from the eye of the hook. I've seen gorgeous emergers that use muskrat fur for the wing case, but so far mine have worked perfectly well for me.

Though I occasionally use an emerger for the duration of a hatch, I usually switch to a standard dry fly once I see trout actually taking winged flies from the surface. There are several styles of dry flies that imitate this stage, the dun stage, of mayflies: thorax flies as popularized by one of my heroes, Vincent Marinaro; cut-winged duns; hackle-point winged duns; comparaduns; and others. There are so many — what's a poor fly-flinger to do? I've settled on comparaduns for the bulk of my fly-fishing to dun hatches of mayflies, mainly because I'm a cheapskate. When Caucci and Nastasi's splendid entomological reference, *Hatches*, appeared, I figured that the comparadun style of dry fly that was introduced in the text was a gimmick to help sell the book. Not so, I discovered. It was Bruce who converted me to the comparadun.

"Rich, they work," he chided, "and since you don't have to hackle them, they're cheap to tie. It's almost like using free flies."

Bruce was correct, of course. After the hook is bought, the body, tailing material, and comparadun wing cost is next to nothing. Though many fly tyers have abandoned the Caucci and Nastasi deer hair wing in favor of elk hair because the elk hair flares more effectively than the hair from a deer mask, I still use the deer hair. If the fly's tails are split, the wing doesn't need to be flared to help support the fly, and, in my opinion, makes a better fly silhoutte.

Comparaduns are durable, too. I regularly fish to hatches of Sulphurs on the Little Shawnee and elsewhere, and it is standard to catch and release 10 to 15 trout on one comparadun. In fact, I usually leave the fly in a fish (or in a tree on my backcast) before it ever wears out.

Comparaduns are really effective, too. When I see a trout take a real dun, I am pretty certain that I can raise him on a comparadun. The exception to this comes on those heavily fished waters that have been overpublicized by kiss-and-tell fishermen. On these challenging rivers and creeks, you might need to have alternative fly styles to imitate dun hatches of mayflies.

On overfished rivers where comparaduns are used regularly, trout that have been caught and released once or twice may snub a comparadun. When that occurs, I generally switch to a hackle-point winged dun or to a cut-winged dun. Sometimes this change will work wonders.

At one time, Bruce and I fished a central Pennsylvania stream in solitude. I'm not allowed to mention the name of this stream in print. However, it doesn't really matter anymore, though: The stream has been popularized by several outdoor writers, and it is usually mobbed these days. Its trout, which would once rise freely to any fraud that even remotely resembled its prevalent Sulphur mayflies, have grown fussy and will often reject even the most artful of imitations. When I visit this stream, which is seldom in recent years, I often have my comparaduns rejected by the now-civilized trout. By changing to another style of Sulphur dun, I can sometimes catch trout that have refused my comparaduns. The first time the trout of this river snubbed my comparaduns, I was aghast and was reluctant to change over. But after an hour of frustration, I did change to a cut-winged dun, and I salvaged my evening. I have come to agree with experts who tell you to carry several styles of duns: On heavily fished trout streams, it's pretty good insurance.

I believe that body color of mayfly duns — and emergers, too — is an important factor in helping to make a fly attractive to the trout. Is color important on comparaduns or standard hackled duns during heavy hatches of mayflies? I think so. I have had too many trout refuse a fly and then take a similar one of a slightly different

Super Sulphurs: Left to right — Nymph, comparadun and spinner.

body color to believe otherwise. On one nearby stream, there is a hatch of Blue-winged Olives. During this hatch, the trout want flies with a light olive body: Dark olive doesn't work well. The undersides of the real flies, the parts that the trout see, are light olive and contribute to the trout's acceptance or rejection of the artificials. I use tan bodies on my Sulphurs because the Sulphurs on the Little Shawnee and other trout streams I fish frequently are more buff-colored than yellow. Anglers on other streams use more yellow in their flies because their Sulphurs are truly sulphur-hued.

Thankfully there are still a few streams that aren't totally pounded to death during the hatches and where the trout aren't so educated that you need a Ph.D. to catch them. Blessedly, a few sections of the Little Shawnee are this way, and the trout take just about any imitation that they see. When I began to tie flies, I didn't put any wings on my dun imitations (because I couldn't), and they worked perfectly well. Though I now wing all my hackle duns because they look nicer than unwinged flies, wings are not necessary to fool unsophisticated trout. My fly boxes still contain some of my relatively ancient flies, and I can take trout on them in places where the fishing pressure is not too heavy. Mainly, though, on these wonderful, unpressured, rare sections of streams, I am content to use my five-cent comparaduns to match hatching mayfly duns.

I suppose the spinner fall, the third major stage of a hatch, is the stage that gave me the most trouble over the years. I tied Female Beaverkills to imitate Sulphur spinners at first but finally realized they didn't work very well because the real flies had extruded their eggs before they hit the water. Perhaps my early problems were due to my not knowing what was occurring, that spinners were adult flies that had molted in streamside trees and bushes and were coming back to the stream to mate, lay eggs, and then to die. The dead flies, floating awash in the surface film, were the ones the trout were taking. Unfortunately for me, my imitations didn't always cut it.

Finally, however, I discovered poly-winged spinners. These no-hackle, flush-floating flies are excellent imitations of dying and dead mayfly spinners. After Dan urged me to give them a shot, my catches during spinner falls improved dramatically. Today, I usually catch my largest trout during hatch periods while I am fishing with spinner imitations.

Mayflies such as Sulphurs spend up to an hour flying out of the trees where they've molted and congregating over riffles during their procreative rites. While in the air mating, they obviously aren't available to the trout. These large clusters of flies slowly but surely sink to the stream's surface, the flies often crashing onto the surface en masse. The trout go absolutely bananas. When I think the trout have begun to rise for spinners, I usually head for slow, flat pools at the base of riffled water. The lunkers in the Little Shawnee and other favorite trout streams hang out there and will readily feed on the bountiful insects. The trout are vulnerable then, and the poly-winged spinners are effective medicine on these feeding trout. Bruce once put me in a position where I caught an 18-inch, a 19-inch, and a 20-inch trout on consecutive casts. This occurred on a public-access northern Pennsylvania trout river. The poly-winged spinner has worked similar feats with smaller trout for me. At any rate, these marvelous little flies account for my largest dry fly-caught trout during most trout seasons. That poly-winged spinners are also five-cent flies to tie is another thing in their favor.

I don't think the color of a mayfly spinner is very important, especially imitations that are used in the fading evening light. I use white poly yarn for the wings of all my mayfly spinners, and these wings are not only effective in helping to create a favorable silhouette of a mayfly spinner, but the white poly wing also helps me to be able to spot the fly in the fading evening light, a factor which certainly helps me to hook up with lots of trout. Nor do I think body color is crucial on a mayfly spinner. Unlike duns, which I think the trout get a good look at, the spinners which fall at dusk often are taken by the trout due to their shape. I agree with the noted fly tyer who once said that 90 percent of all mayflies can be matched by poly-winged spinners with rust-colored bodies, though I think cream mayflies and the little, dark *Tricorythodes* mayflies are exceptions to this.

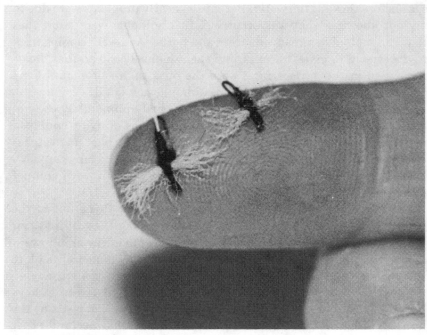

*A pair of **Tricorythodes** mayflies.*

The spinner falls cause the most intense feeding of all during a mayfly hatch. Duns, which often hatch over a period of hours, are available to trout in variable numbers over a relatively long period of time in many cases. The spinners, however, which fall to the stream all at once, are available in these large numbers for only a short period of time most evenings. The trout certainly know this, and they feed frenziedly to gather in as many flies as they can. I sometimes see trout hovering just under the surface during spinner falls as they use as little energy as possible to gather in the dead mayflies. Since an imitation is competing with so many naturals for the attention of a trout, it sometimes takes four or five casts to present your fly to a trout which is actively feeding and may rise to a real fly at about the time your imitation gets to him. Be persistent: You can generally fool a trout that is actively rising to spinners.

Pay particular attention to trout that are rising near cover. These are often the big ones. When I find a softly rising fish on the Little Shawnee that is near a log jam or a brush pile, I check my tippet for frays and the fly hook for sharpness. I want to assure myself that I am prepared to deal with larger than average trout in such situations. Through carelessness, I have lost too many large trout in the past.

Dan Deters kneels by Falling Spring Branch during a Trico hatch.

Fly-fishing experts agree it is best to approach trout from downstream.

There is a hole on the Little Shawnee that has surrendered several trout of 18 to 20 inches to me over the years. It's a perfect lunker hideout. The pool is fed from a nice riffle where mayfly spinners like to congregate. On the left bank (facing upstream), there is a large willow tree. The stream has carved a deep hole under its roots, and big trout live there. Unfortunately, erosion is slowly undermining the tree, and I suspect that spring floods will soon wash it away, as they have with several other sentinel willows. But for now, it is a real lunker hole. It is easy to fish, too. On the bank opposite the willow is an open pasture.

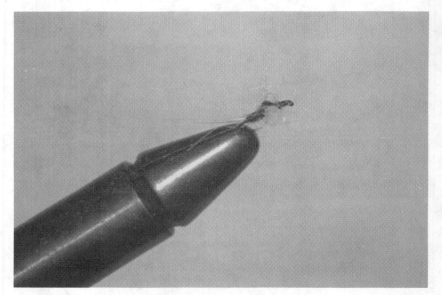

A Trico spinner works well in midsummer.

The first large trout I landed there was rising along the edge of the roots near a foam line during a Sulphur spinner fall. He sucked in my little poly-winged spinner without hesitation, and the battle was on. I figured to lose him under the roots, but the roots must not extend into the water very far: I have never been broken-off under this particular willow. I beached this trout five minutes or so after I hooked him. He was one of the first 19-inch brown trout I ever caught on the Shawnee. That he wasn't 20 inches was a major disappointment at the time: I hadn't yet caught the trout at the walnut tree. Even so, I was really delighted with him and with my discovery of the pool.

My most recent lunker from the willow pool came in August during a light hatch of cream mayflies. I had on a cream poly-winged spinner that hot, humid evening. This trout even fought sluggishly. It was more of a pull against dead weight than a real battle, and it probably took less than five minutes to land the big trout. Despite the lackluster fight, this trout was the heaviest I've ever taken from the willow pool: a shade under 20 inches but so heavy that I couldn't get both my hands even close to going around the big brown's body! I would guess his weight at four pounds, a huge trout on the little creek. Pools such as this willow pool are prime locations for big trout, and I try to end most evenings of fishing to mayfly hatches in such locations. They have produced well for me.

The author regularly fishes three fly styles during mayfly hatches: an emerging/floating nymph during the early stage of the hatches; a dun to imitate the hatching sub-adults; and a poly-winged spinner to imitate the dying egg layers.

One other thing needs to be noted about hatch fishing. In warm weather, the duns of Sulphurs and other mayflies emerge concurrently with the spinner fall. Though most trout will take both duns and spinners at such times, sometimes trout will feed selectively on either the dun or the spinner stage. Dun imitations often work better in broken water while spinners produce better in the flats when this occurs. However, this is a generalization: You have to be observant to be sure which type of flies a selective trout is taking, especially at dusk. Usually when I encounter a hatch and spinner fall occurring simultaneously, as often happens during late-spring Sulphur emergences, I head for the flat pools and knot on a spinner. As I've noted, that is when and how I usually catch my largest trout during mayfly activity.

In summary, I regularly fish three fly styles when I fish for trout during mayfly hatches: an emerging/floating nymph during the early stage of the hatch; a dun to imitate the hatching sub-adults; and a poly-winged spinner to imitate the dying egg layers. This strategy works well for me and accounts for a lot of lovely trout.

Chapter 12

A STOLEN TROUT

One summer afternoon in the mid-1980s I had decided to fish a lovely wooded section of Canoe Creek. This was in the days before I finally decided it really wasn't worthwhile to fish there anymore due to beavers' dams warming the water, causing an invasion of pickerel from the downstream Department of Environmental Resources lake. At the time I was still hopeful that the stream could sustain its wild trout population.

Anyhow, I was doing reasonably well for a mid-afternoon foray, having caught and released several decent trout, though they were nearly all stocked fish. One, however, had been a 16-inch holdover brown trout I was still gloating about when I arrived at a long, flat pool that was shaded by mature hemlocks which had somehow survived the gypsy moth onslaught. There were several trout rising in the pool, and I was confident that they would take the Grizzly Parachute I was using. No way!

Five minutes and a dozen casts over each fish later, I knew that these trout weren't going to be suckered in by the trusty fish finder that had worked so well in the downstream pockets and runs. I sat down and cut off the little parachute as I tried to decide what to do. Suddenly I spotted a tiny plop in the pool, and seconds later a trout rose a foot or two downstream. I told myself to knot on a size 16 Crowe Beetle: These fish were feeding on beetles that were tumbling out of the hemlock at the head of the pool.

The author works his way upstream to locate and capture some trout.

I am not a great fan of bug fishing: Ants and beetles are difficult to see on the water, especially in shaded areas. But they do work, and I often use them to take fussy midsummer trout I find feeding in flat pools. I like beetles better than ants because they make little splashes when they land in the water. This attracts the attention of nearby trout. It also lets me know just where my fly is on the water.

Anyhow, my first plop of the beetle over the closest trout resulted in a confident rise from the trout but a clumsy reaction from me, resulting in a missed trout. "Darn it!" I muttered disgustedly.

I pitched the little beetle to the next trout, and a minute later I had a stocked 12-inch brown trout ready to release. Meanwhile, the first trout began to rise again, and after I'd released the 12-incher, I directed another cast toward the trout I'd missed. This time I set the hook solidly when he engulfed the little beetle, and not long afterwards I had a 10-inch rainbow in hand. However, the little rainbow was bleeding badly, having been hooked in the gills somehow.

Now, I dislike killing trout and would have released this one if I had thought it had any chance of recovery. But the fish was nearly dead already, and it would have been less ethical to try to release it than to take it home. I laid it in a little puddle beside me as I decided to try for the third and final riser in the pool. In all honesty, I was going to keep this fish, too, if I caught him. I figured it would take two trout this size to make a trout dinner for Donna, Bobby, and me.

This trout, too, rose confidently, but I merely pricked him when he rose for the beetle. I was only mildly upset, knowing I would pick up another trout for the meal as I continued to fish.

Since no more trout were feeding in this pool, I reached to pick up the little rainbow to clean it. However, he had nearly disappeared. Only his head remained in the little puddle: The rest of him had vanished underneath some stones. I didn't think much about it until I grasped the trout's head. I figured the trout had somehow drifted under the stones.

However, when I grasped the trout, something abruptly jerked it out of my hand, pulling the trout completely out of sight underneath the rocks of the puddle! I was more than a little shocked and jumped up. What the heck's going on here? I wondered.

I decided to retrieve the vanishing trout by pulling rocks from the edge of the puddle until I could see it. Five minutes and many stones later, I'd not recovered the trout. It had completely disappeared!

Where had it gone? Had it somehow recovered and swum into an underwater sanctuary? I doubt it. Had a gremlin stolen the trout? I don't think so. Then what happened?

Though I cannot be certain, I believe an opportunistic water snake was hidden in the stones and stole the first trout I'd decided to take home in years. No matter what stole the trout, it was a brief, startling episode that remains one of the strangest occurrences I've experienced in my 20-plus years as a trout fisherman.

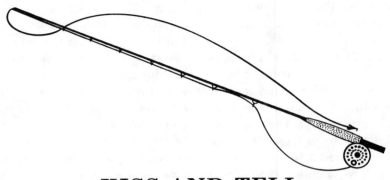

Chapter 13

KISS-AND-TELL
FISHERMEN, 1990

"...fly-fishing in its best form, in the best circumstances, is a rather secretive and solitary kind of sport."
                        - Vincent Marinaro - *A Modern Dry Fly Code*

Not too long ago, Bruce and I had gone to a nearby fly shop to stock up. I was worshipping the wall of gorgeous Metz necks when Bruce suddenly interrupted my reverie. "Hey, Rich, did you hear that old 'so-and-so' is writing another book?"

"That's nice. I hope it's a lot better than his other ones. They contradict some other stuff he has written and said," I replied, taking my eyes off the gorgeous necks momentarily.

"It's gonna be worse. He's writing about our state's trout streams and about their fly hatches. Knowing him, he'll give exact directions to every good hole he knows about. Heck, he'll probably even include maps. He has even asked guys around here to fish with him and to help him tell about our favorite little creeks," Bruce continued. "I suppose he'll find someone, too, though nobody I know is willing to help him tell the world about our favorite streams."

This man is what Robert Traver used to call a "kiss-and-tell fisherman." The kiss-and-tell fishermen have to tell about every creek they ever fish. Afterwards, hordes rush in and overfish the stream.

Why despise kiss-and-tell fishermen? They spoil good trout fishing, especially for anglers who must spend most of their time fishing close to home. Their articles praising the fishing on certain streams gets the juices flowing in their readers, and hordes of traveling anglers descend upon once uncrowded trout streams, destroying the solitude and fine angling that had formerly been found there.

One example comes to mind immediately. A certain creek in a certain state once provided uncrowded, fantastic fly-fishing in a bucolic setting. Trout of 12 to 15 inches were average, and it was disappointing if a trout of 17 inches or better wasn't brought to net. Word began to get out, of course, and the stream's fishing pressure was gradually increasing. However, it remained the best trout stream I had ever seen until I made a dream trip to Wyoming and Montana.

But one summer one of the kiss-and-tellers discovered the stream and publicized it in an article in a national magazine, describing the creek as being underfished. The result was — and still is — a catastrophe. During hatches of its prevalent mayflies, it is difficult to find a 100-yard stretch that isn't being pounded. The fishing experience there is a mere shadow of the way it once was.

A certain trout stream in a certain state boasts a terrific hatch of *Tricorythodes* mayflies. Introduced to this fishing by a friend who swore me to secrecy, I enjoyed several seasons of splendid dry-fly fishing there. Unfortunately, one of the kiss-and-tell fishermen discovered the creek, wrote it up in a couple of his columns, and helped to destroy the solitude that had formerly been found there. During Trico hatches, the creek now boasts about as many anglers as a stocked stream has on opening day.

The quality of a fishing experience is obviously diminished by overcrowded conditions. Montana's Bighorn River offers some of the most splendid fly-fishing I've ever seen, yet overpublicity has caused some serious problems on the Bighorn. I have read about drift boats running over wading anglers, anglers cursing other fishermen, and even fist fights between competitive fishermen. From personal experience, I know that it would have been easy to cause problems with other anglers on the crowded sections of the Bighorn I fished.

Kiss-and-tell fishermen also contribute to diminished stocks of trout in rivers they write about. Take central Pennsylvania's Little Juniata River. This river could be one of the country's best trophy trout streams, but it isn't. It has an excellent food base for the trout, some wonderful fly hatches, and good water quality. When it first began to be a viable trout fishery in the mid-1970s, it was producing good numbers of large trout, too. But not anymore, at least in the numbers that the river could support.

Why not? Quite a few angling writers — and I am one of them — have praised the Little Juniata in print, luring anglers to it. The river is open to fishing the year around, with an eight-trout limit from mid-April to Labor Day and a three-trout limit the rest of the year. There are no tackle restrictions. The minimum size is seven inches from April to September, nine inches the rest of the year. Consequently, the anglers drawn to the river by the articles singing the praises of the Little Juniata can and do creel just about every trout they catch. Had the Little Juniata been developed with slot limits or some catch-and-release areas before the scribes over publicized it, its fishing would doubtlessly be significantly better than it is today. It would take some real courage to establish more restrictive regulations for the Little Juniata, and it is not likely to be done. Thus, most of its trout will consist of eight- to 11-inch fish.

As Robert Traver, one of my angler-writer heroes, penned years ago, it is difficult to imagine how kiss-and-tell fishermen maintain any friendships. Most good flyrodders I know are pretty close-mouthed and try to protect their favorite fishing holes. It's tough to find quality trout fishing these days. As Traver noted, I think it is a real compliment when another angler shows you one of his favorite uncrowded spots. There aren't many around.

Kiss-and-tell fishermen can spoil good trout streams with lavish praise. They can also contribute to diminished stocks of trout, especially on smaller streams that have no regulations.

When Bruce or one of my other friends shows me a secret hot spot, I generally have to promise not to write about it. It is a promise I gladly keep.

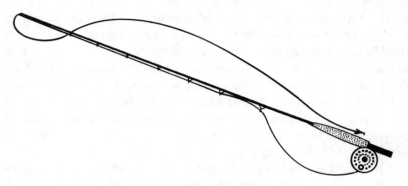

Chapter 14

LESS FREQUENTLY USED
FISHING STRATEGIES

Over the years, I've come to rely on fishing to mayfly hatches and fishing to the water for about 90 to 95 percent of my fly-fishing. Unlike many flyrodders from other areas, I do not get to fish to a lot of caddis hatches, nor do I do a lot of bug fishing. Still, I do manage to fish to an occasional caddis hatch and find enough trout rising for terrestrials that I've had to come up with some workable tactics for these situations.

My strategy in fishing to caddis hatches is very similar to the strategy I use in fishing to mayfly hatches. Though I have occasionally fished with deep caddis imitations, I have enjoyed most of my success during caddis hatches on or near the surface.

Most of the caddisfly hatches I have run into are hatches of grayish or tan flies. The bodies of these flies have varied from gray to green with several shades of gray-green in between. Therefore, I have come to rely on two basic colors of caddis imitations: dun caddisses with muskrat fur bodies and tan (ginger) caddisses with olive bodies.

When I see trout beginning to take hatching caddisses, I generally tie on a Wright Caddis of the appropriate color, hoping for surface action. I often twitch the fly as it approaches an actively feeding trout, a "sudden inch" as Leonard Wright aptly called it. This is something I do not do when I am fishing a Wright Caddis to the water. If I am fortunate, I'll raise about 75 percent of the trout I see breaking the surface and will enjoy spirited action. I prefer to fish this way for the duration of a caddisfly hatch when possible. However, it's not always possible.

About half the time, the trout are taking emerging caddisses just under the surface film, and I have to use my version of Gary LaFontaine's sparkle pupa. I've found that a light green body works well most of the time. It gets darker when it gets wet, either from the water or from the saliva I wet it with to sink it. I use dark hair from a deer mask for the wingcase and do not hackle the fly at all. It is a workable pattern. I dead drift my first cast or two with this fly over the trout, hoping for takes. This works about half the time, but if a dead drift fails to raise a trout, I will then twitch this fly as it approaches the feeding fish. This can result in explosive takes, and I often break off fish on the strike because the splashy rises get me excited, and I pull too hard.

During the actual emergence of caddisflies, I prefer to fish downstream when practical. Fishing downstream permits me to control my line and leader so that I can give my fly the quick twitch it often needs to provoke strikes. The caddis hatches I encounter usually last about an hour to two hours, and I generally catch six to 15 trout in this time, depending on how many trout are showing and how heavy the hatch is.

I have read much about caddis mating and egg-laying behavior, but the caddis egg-laying I have observed is basically of a nature similar to a mayfly spinner fall, though I have yet to encounter one as heavy as a spinner fall of mayflies. Anyhow, being relatively unimaginative as a fly tyer, I usually use the same fly as I use for the emerging pupae to imitate dead caddisses: my version of LaFontaine's sparkle emerger. Fished dead drift, flush in the surface, this fly works perfectly well for me in most situations. When I encounter caddisses that are flopping around before dying, I use an elk-hair caddis, which rides higher than the hackleless fly. Though I don't purposely twitch it, the elk-hair caddis with its palmered hackle seems to have enough movement on its own to attract trout which are feeding on dying caddisflies that still have some kick in them.

I do not have any experience dealing with caddisflies that dive underwater to lay their eggs, and I don't really know how I'd handle imitating them. I realize that caddis hatches overshadow mayfly hatches in many places, but on the streams I fish, it's the other way around.

During the trout season, I also run into situations where I find trout rising in the absence of hatches. In my formative years as a flyrodder,

The author works to get a trout close enough to net.

these trout were safe from me: I just couldn't catch them. As I grew older, a midge would occasionally take one, but my success with these frustrating trout was certainly inconsistent at best. One of my readings of A Modern Dry Fly Code set the bells ringing in my head: These trout were taking terrestrial bugs, probably ants, and that winter I whipped up a bunch of size 16 and 18 black fur ants. I cleverly used a dun hackle for their legs so that I could spot the little ants floating over the fish.

The next summer I dealt pretty effectively with the majority of flat-water risers I encountered. Today, as I merrily fish along with a caddis or a Grizzly Parachute and come upon a riser in a pool that ignores my fish finder, I confidently clip off the fly and replace it with a fur ant. Seven or eight times out of 10 this will fool the rising trout.

For a good many years I wrote off the other 20-30 percent of these flatwater feeders. I reasoned that they were just too tough for me to spend any time on. My attitude about that, however, experienced a severe jolt one morning now nine or 10 years in the past on an excursion Dan Deters and I made on the small branch of the Little Shawnee. We ran into a trout feeding at the base of a large willow.

"Try him," Dan told me.

"I don't know. That looks like one of those trout that won't take my ant," I replied, but I went ahead and tried him. The fish totally ignored my fly.

"Your turn," I told Dan, who had knotted something onto his tippet while I fished.

I watched Dan, who's normally a good caster, plop his fly onto the creek. I figured his poor presentation would terrify the feeding trout. Not so. That trout engulfed the fly, and moments later Dan had a fat wild brown about a foot long ready to release.

"Let me see your fly," I commanded, and when I reached for it, I discovered a mass of frazzled black deer hair attached to his hook. "What's this? A deer hair monster?"

Dan chuckled. "No, Rich, it was a Crowe Beetle. They're easy to tie, and they take trout that are rising in the flat pools in midsummer."

I was properly chagrined. Here was Dan, supposedly my pupil, giving me another one of the many lessons he's taught me about fly-fishing.

That day I went home and tied up a dozen of the easy-to-tie beetles in a half hour. All you have to do is bind some black deer hair to a size 14 or 16 dry fly hook, bend it forward from the bend, and tie it off just behind the eye of the hook. It is so simple to tie that its lack of durability is a minor inconvenience. The Crowe Beetle accounts for

Fly-fishing can often turn from a mild interest to an intense passion.

most of the rest of 20-30 percent of flatwater risers I find in midsummer.

Ants and beetles are the mainstays of my bug box, but one other terrestrial has earned a place in my box over the years: Ed Shenk's Letort Cricket. I don't use it often, but when I do, it generally attracts the trout I'm after. I tie it in size 18 for early summer and size 12 for later on. It's rare for me to use the smaller version, but the larger one sees service reasonably regularly, especially for trout I find rising softly along log jams, tree roots, or undercut banks during midsummer. These trout are often of good size, too.

One of my most embarrassing fishing moments occurred years ago on the Letort while I was using a cricket. I'd hooked a large trout that had weeded up, and I couldn't pull him loose. To get out to the weeds, I'd have had to wade in over my hip boots, which I do often enough by accident and certainly did not want to do on purpose. As no one else was around, I laid down my rod, took off my boots, stripped down, and then picked up the rod and waded out to the spot where the fish had wrapped me in the weeds. I gave a slight tug on the leader to raise the trout from the weeds, but he was gone. As I waded back to my boots and pile of clothes, Bruce and another angler appeared.

"What are you doing, Rich? Skinny-dipping?" Bruce laughed as I retrieved my clothes.

As I put them on and started to explain, Bruce and the other angler were laughing so hard that I couldn't get in my explanation. It was something I didn't live down for a long time. But if I had caught that trout, I wouldn't have cared at all.

That I don't have more to say about fishing during caddis hatches or fishing with bugs is a result of my fishing experiences. There aren't many caddis hatches on the streams I fish regularly, and I don't have to use terrestrials very often to ensure success while astream. But when I do encounter these situations, the tactics I've described do work quite well.

Chapter 15

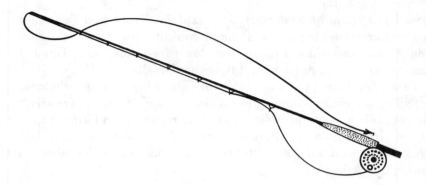

THE FIRST FLY-FISHERMAN

The literature of fly-fishing extends far into the past. The English wrote extensively about the sport, with Izaak Walton coming to be regarded as "Father Izaak," almost a patron saint to the angling fraternity. However, Walton's *The Compleat Angler's* additions to the annals of fly-fishing were contributed by another angler-writer, Charles Cotton, and it seems that Cotton's writing were based on an even earlier work by Dame Juliana Berners, the Abbess of Sopwell in England. In her work, *The Treatise of Fishing with an Angle*, which was included in an early book about the outdoors, *The Book of St. Albans*, she gave descriptions of angling methods and the equipment that was employed. This suggests that fly-fishing had been around for quite some time. Berners gave dressings for 12 flies, with advice about how to use the flies, too, which is just like having an early *Streamside Guide!*

If Berners' 1496 contribution to the literature of fly-fishing is not historical enough, then one must return to the ancients for some mention of fly-fishing. Generally, Aelian, who lived in the late 200s B.C., is credited for being the first to describe the act of using artificials to catch fish. He describes the concocting of a Macedonian fly tied with a red body and two waxy-colored feathers from a rooster to catch the speckled fish (trout?) which fed upon the real flies. The fish rising to these artificial flies enjoyed a bitter repast, according to Aelian.

Perhaps, though, if translators of another ancient, Martial, who preceded Aelian by a couple hundred years, are accurate, the literature of fly-fishing began with the following:

"Who has not seen the scarus rise,
Decoyed and killed by fraudful flies?"

And so the literature of fly-fishing has come from antiquity to the present day, much of it describing the pleasures of fly-fishing experiences, much of it describing the tactics and the tools that are useful to the flyrodder. However, none of the literature has been able to trace the roots of fly-fishing to its source, perhaps because angling scholars were content to believe that the writings of Aelian or perhaps Martial were the first to deal with the subject.

I, too, accepted the findings of the angling historians who had decreed that these early writers were the fathers of fly-fishing, or at least fly-fishing literature, that is, until I received a visit from my neighbor, Dr. Archie O. Logist, a science professor at the nearby Ganister Technical Institute, not many years ago. He is responsible for the shattering of my former illusions about the origins of fly-fishing.

It all began one evening after I'd had a dandy outing on the Little Shawnee. The trout had risen well, and I was returning triumphantly after having duped a dozen of them with a small mayfly mimic. I hoped these trout would become a little wiser after their experience at the end of a fly line and would be a little harder to fool the next time. However, knowing the foolish ways of trout, I smugly figured I could catch them again if I wanted to.

I had just pulled into my garage and was gathering my paraphernalia from the back of my old Scout when the evening quiet was shattered by a piercing scream. I jumped and would have flown at east 10 feet in the air, but stopped abruptly when I hit my head on the rear door latch. The gear in my arms flew all over the driveway upon my return to earth as I searched the night for the hobgoblin I knew was about to attack me. As my eyes darted from bush to bush, I discovered, to my immense relief, that the sound had not emanated from a supernatural night creature but rather from the diminutive professor of phenomenology.

"Holy cripes, Arch what's the matter?" I asked angrily, knowing full well that the little professor was normally a sedate fellow. He was certainly not one to come flying through the night frightening innocent fly-fishermen. "You nearly scarced me out of my BVDs!"

"Rich, I've made an important discovery!" he cried. "I just found some ancient paintings in a cave at the old stone quarry along Little Shawnee Creek while I was spelunking. They're the first cave paintings ever found in this area!"

105

"Spe-what?" I muttered as I gathered up my fishing gear.

"Cave exploring," he began. "I know you think you aren't interested, Rich, but I think you would be. Some of the art seems to be about fishing."

"Oh?" I responded with little enthusiasm. "What does that have to do with me?"

"I want to photograph my discovery. As I said, this is the first cave art found in this area. I need your help."

"Why don't you get one of your friends at the college to help you?" I responded.

"Because they would want to take credit for the find. I want someone who doesn't care about the cave to help me so that I receive full academic honors for the discovery.

Now, I'm not really smart, but I didn't want to crawl around a cave. "Look, Arch, I'm not going to go into some crummy cave and get all muddy. I . . . ."

"Sure you are, Rich! Remember the time I came over and fixed your television set before the NCAA basketball championship? You said you'd be glad to do me a favor when I asked, and I'd like to collect tomorrow morning at 7:00. I'll stop for you after breakfast."

This is typical brown trout water. Brown trout can lie here in their leisure and feed well. (Photo courtesy Paul Tofte)

Trapped! Again my mechanical ineptitude had backed me into a corner. I had often sworn my hatred for telephones and lawn mowers, but this was the first time a television set had betrayed me. I had to agree to Arch's demand to be ready at 7:00.

True to his word, Archie arrived punctually at the appointed hour, and I had to rush my morning coffee with me, spilling half of it as I crawled into his van. As we proceeded out of town, he spoke in educated, scientific terms about the values the cave paintings might possess, but only minutes out of town, I fell asleep. He woke me up when he parked the van, and when we got out, he handed me some silly little hammers, a tripod, and a camera. He strapped on a knapsack and carried some kind of long stick. We traveled up the face of a small rock wall for about a hundred yards where we abruptly halted. I glanced quizzically at my guide.

"We're here," he announced.

"We're where?" I queried.

"At the cave," he responded triumphantly. "Look at that limestone ledge. About two feet to the right of that big rock is the cave entrance."

All I could see was an oversized groundhog hole. "I'm not going in there!" I announced with firm resolve.

"Don't be ridiculous; you certainly are!" replied the junior-league Sir Edmund Hillary, and with a not-too-gentle shove, he pushed me toward the hole.

I skidded to the hole, and he told me to get going. Being fed up with the entire escapade, I figured I might as well get it over with, and I hunkered down and crawled headfirst through a slimy, narrow tunnel for about 15 or 20 feet. At the end of the tunnel, I found myself in a large cave room. When I switched on my flashlight, I could see that the room was about 10 feet long, 10 feet wide, and 15 feet high. When Archie arrived, he told me that our flashlights did not illuminate the cave well enough, and he told me to stay put while he went for more lights. He was back in a jiffy, and in a couple of minutes he had the room shining like a glittering ballroom. Stalagmites and stalactites — I don't know one from the other — extended from floor to ceiling. There was a steady dripping of water, and I zipped my light nylon jacket as I gazed at the underground marvels. I had all but forgotten about the mission when he said, "Look here, Rich."

I glanced at a dark wall which the good professor was examining, and it was then that I noticed the paintings on the walls. They were done in red, brown, green and blue and seemed to tell stories of cave life and of hunting.

"Where's the fishing painting?" I remembered.

He stepped aside and pointed to a sequence of small drawings bracketed by a deer and a colorful fish. It was easy to tell that the fish represented a gaudy brook trout and that some of the pictures in the series showed a caveman fishing. But the picture of the deer and several of the others seemed to have little to do with fishing.

"What do you make of it, Rich?"

"Well, it's easy to tell that the guy was a fisherman. Some of the paintings show him kneeling and casting, and the very last one shows the brook trout he was fishing for. He used a lot of red and green paint to color it. Heck, maybe he was even a fly-fisherman like I am," I laughed.

But my laugher died instantly: I froze on the spot as I glued my eyes to the sequence of paintings. No, it just couldn't be true. As I have noted, I had read the accounts of Aelian and Martial. True, the writers who had discussed these ancients had hinted that fly-fishing roots might be deeper still, but until this instant I had given these hints no thought.

"Rich! Rich!" Dr. Logist yelled as he shook me. "What's wrong? Are you all right?"

"Arch!" I screamed — returning his cry of the previous evening. "This is incredible! These paintings are even more important than you thought! They'll revolutionize the whole history of fly-fishing!"

"Settle down," he commanded, though cynically, perhaps thinking of my earlier attitude about the expedition. When I'd regained my composure, he said, "Now, tell me about it."

"Well, Arch. Let's call the caveman in the painting 'Grog.' Grog was a fly-fisherman."

"Oh? And just how did you decide that? I thought you said some of the paintings were not even about fishing?"

"That's true," I conceded. "At first, I didn't understand the whole sequence. But now I think I've got it figured out."

"Well, tell me about it."

"Okay. The deer painting represents a deer that Grog killed one day when he was out hunting. The next one shows him taking some of the deer's hair while his wife was tanning the hide. Do you follow me so far?"

"Yes."

"Good. The next pictures of those brownish fish represent the baitfish that live in the Little Shawnee — almost the same color as the deer hair. As you probably know, cavemen had made crude hooks from stone that they used to catch fish. Well, this caveman must have been pretty smart — at least by caveman standards — and he reasoned that he could create a fake minnow out of the deer hair. The picture of him sitting down with the hair in one hand and that little thing in the other shows him trying to make a bucktail type fly to imitate the brown minnows."

"Fascinating, go on," said my neighbor, now concentrating on my every word.

"Well, the problem for Grog was to figure out a way to bind the deer hair to the hook," I told him.

The next couple drawings showed Grog watching his wife sewing clothes and showed a vine growing outside a cave door. The painting that followed these showed Grog fishing a pool on the Little Shawnee. It wasn't difficult to decipher the meaning of these: Grog had seen his wife using animal sinews to sew animal hides together to make clothes, so he reasoned that he could use sinews to attach the deer hair to his hook. But it didn't work because the sinews were too thick. So Grog used long, hairlike creepers from the troublesome vine that grew outside his cave entrance.

I continued the narrative. I said, "Hooks didn't have eyes — holes to put a line through in a fishing hook — in those days; so Grog carefully tied a long sinew to his hook which he then attached to a long oak branch. He went down to the creek, and being an experienced worm fisherman, he cut a forked stick — see it in this drawing — and he propped his rod on it and floated the crude fly toward a favorite trout lair, those tree roots in that drawing. But nothing happened, and even though he now knew that there was a flaw in his plan, he had to return to the cave. Even the wives of cavemen would tolerate only so much fishing.

"Grog kept at it, though, but he constantly failed and resorted to bait fishing. But as the drawing right here shows, Grog came upon a solution as he was falling asleep one afternoon after watching minnows in a small pool. Now, he realized that his minnow sank to the bottom after it was waterlogged, but his drowned deer hair did not dart around like the real minnows did when they intercepted a morsel of food. The real minnows attracted the attention of the trout when they moved! A sick minnow was easily noticed by a predator and was almost always attacked. Thus, Grog realized if he made his minnow creation move like it was hurt or was feeding, the trout would attack it.

"With this in mind, Grog retrieved his fly, and he then tossed it toward the willow roots. However, this time he did not rest his rod on a forked stick but rather kept his fishing line tight and tried to jiggle the fly to make it look alive. That was all it took. Out of the tangle erupted a hungry trout, it smashed the fly, and Grog immediately lifted the pole to set the hook. He had to pressure the fish to tire it by advancing and retreating along the bank as the trout made its fight. After all, Grog did not have a fishing reel to release and gather line as I do. But he was agile enough to be able to move along the creek at the fish's speed, and after a five-minute tussle, he beached the fine brook trout.

"Grog repeated his ruse in several more pools that afternoon, and when he returned to the cave, he presented his catch to his wife, who was certainly delighted. The fish were all trout — none of those bony suckers like Grog caught on worms. Grog was able to repeat his success with the deer flies any time he wanted after that; he had truly become a trout specialist.

"And that, Arch, is how Grog became the world's first fly-fisherman."

"Well, that is remarkable!" said the good doctor. "Did you know that cavemen fly-fished?"

"No, and neither did anyone else. The caveman who made these paintings was the world's first fly-fisherman."

"Good heavens! This discovery is a 'first' in a lot of ways! We'll be famous! Let's set up the cameras."

After the photo session, we hurried out to the van so that no one else would find "our" cave. Upon arriving at home, I told Donna about the adventure and immediately began to chronicle it. This was a number of years ago now. Then why haven't you read about it before?

When Archie and I returned to the cave a week later, we found that the quarry had been reopened and that blasting had obliterated the cave. Still, Dr. Logist's photographs should have substantiated our story.

However, when the film returned from the developer, we found that not even one photo had turned out. There must have been a camera malfunction.

When I tried to tell a couple of my friends about the discovery, they insisted that I had been hitting the sauce, that there was never a cave in the Little Shawnee Creek quarry. In addition, Professor Archie O. Logist was discredited professionally after he had reported the discovery to several professional societies and was then unable to prove his claims. He eventually lost his job at Ganister Tech and moved away.

Nevertheless, I am setting this story on paper so that my fellow feather and fur flingers will no longer blindly accept tales about a Greek being the world's first fly-fisherman. The genesis of fly-fishing has American roots! Grog the caveman, using a deer hair streamer on the Little Shawnee Creek, was actually the world's first fly-fisherman.

Chapter 16

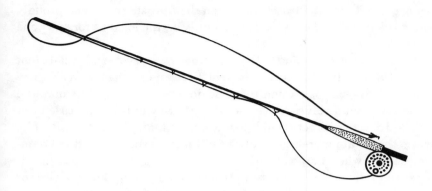

RESISTING TEMPTATION

We fly-fishermen are notorious for collecting relics of our sport. Some of us collect as many books as we can about fly-fishing, others stash away old flyreels, and many more accumulate vintage bamboo flyrods.

Although I have acquired a modest library of fly-fishing tomes, I have accumulated these in my quest for knowledge about the various nuances of the sport, not for the sake of accumulation. At one time, I had also collected 15 years' worth of *Fly Fisherman* and *Trout* magazines.

"Why don't you throw out those old magazines?" Donna frequently asked me. "They're just dust collectors, and they certainly take up a lot of space in your fly tying room."

She was right about the space they required, but knowing the acquisitive nature of flyrodders, I figured they'd come in useful someday. They did, too. Not very long ago I packed up this collection of old magazines and shipped them off to a book dealer. In return, he sent me nine new books about fly-fishing that I just had to have. These books take up far less space in my fly tying room than the dusty old magazines did, though I must confess that the room looked kind of barren for a while.

I guess that the most serious temptation for a fly-fisherman is a desire to accumulate a set of fine split bamboo flyrods. Most of us absolutely drool at the mere thought of old split bamboo flyrods, and the actual sight of one makes us candidates for a dribble cup. Owning one of the beautiful symbols of our sport is almost a universal goal among the fly-fishing fraternity. Even the fly-fisherman who proudly possess a fine bamboo flyrod is constantly on the lookout for "just one more."

In my own case, I am the proud owner of a seven-and-a-half-foot Orvis Battenkill rod. Having bought it for more than a week's pay many years ago, it is a wand that I seldom use because of its material and sentimental values. I even squirrel it away in its metal case most of the time to protect it, only occasionally taking it out to worship. Even then, I am more than a little careful to be sure that I don't damage it. And when I do fish with it — oh my! I stick to the open meadows, and I don't dare to pressure fish with it as I would with a glass or graphite stick. Yet, fishing with the Battenkill is a special treat: The whole rod works fluently, almost sensuously, as I cast to feeding trout. I've often thought it would be nice to have a cane rod as my working rod, one I could use on a regular basis.

Knowing that I want a bamboo flyrod to use regularly, you'll understand how difficult it was for me to avoid an extremely inviting offer a half dozen years ago. Dr. Archie O. Logist, my next-door neighbor at the time, arrived at my kitchen door after I had come home from a trout fishing excursion. Archie walked through the door, holding a gorgeous split bamboo flyrod. "Is it worth anything?" he asked. "A fellow at the institute found it in his basement and wants to sell it. Interested?"

"Sure," I said, craftily calculating how I'd come up with a couple hundred bucks it was no doubt worth. "Let me see it. How much does he want?"

I lovingly caressed the heavy three-piece, nine-foot cane. It was, no doubt, intended for use on large rivers, probably salmon or steelhead rivers, not the small valley creeks and mountain freestone brooks I most often visit. Even so, I wanted the rod if I could get it for a price that wouldn't wreck my marriage.

"$50," the professor replied.

Oh, Lord, $50! I almost gagged with greed. Even though the rod was not one of the big name rods, the fact that it had "South Bend" stamped on its butt helped me to realize that it possessed considerable value. Fifty dollars would be a real steal! I asked myself whether I wanted the rod badly enough to take advantage of the situation. I could not use this rod as my working rod, but there was no doubt in my mind that I could trade it for a rod I could use. But, did I really want this bamboo rod so badly? Should I cheat Archie's friend? My glass and graphite rods work perfectly well on my favorite trout streams.

"Arch, I think that rod's worth a lot more than $50," I finally told him as I went to the fridge for a bottle of beer. "Here, you drink this while I go upstairs and get you a couple addresses."

I came back downstairs and gave him the addresses and phone numbers of two reputable fly tackle dealers in the area. "Tell your friend to call one of these places. They will be able to appraise the rod fairly."

After Arch left with the rod, I experienced that miserable feeling of great loss that you get when something fine has slipped through your fingers, even though I knew I'd done the right thing. I felt even worse a couple days later when Archie told me his friend had been offered an exorbitant sum for the rod, sight unseen, by one of the dealers I'd recommended. I told myself that I'd resisted temptation, that I really didn't want that rod anyhow. What a lie! That rod could have done a lot for me. It could've brought me some big bucks! It could've been bartered for a working rod! It could've... Oh, how I wailed!

Only a couple years after finding out about the value of the old South Bend rod, I was again faced with a decision regarding a cane rod. This rod, however, would have made a fine working rod. One of my students (I've survived 20 years of high school teaching) arrived in class, a smile on his face. "You're a fly-fisherman, Mr. Tate. Want to buy an old flyrod?"

"I doubt it. Let's see it," I said, thinking he was trying to pawn off a cheapo glass stick.

He drew a lovely seven-and-a-half-foot flyrod from a beat-up old tube. The rod was beautiful, a soft yellow color, though during one of its refinishings the brand name had been removed. Still, an expert could figure out its brand from the unusual fittings. Needless to say, I began to salivate when I saw it. "How much?" I asked.

"Twenty bucks. I need some money to fix up my car."

Oh, Lord — $20! Temptation had once again reared its ugly head. I knew the rod wasn't as valuable as the other one had been, but this price was just unbelievable. And besides, I'd be cheating one of my students, and I don't like them to cheat in my classes. Still, it was a dandy rod.

"I'll give you a couple addresses tomorrow," I told him, trying to hide my anguish. "I'm sure you can get a lot more than $20 for a beautiful rod like this."

And I was right. He was offered a substantial sum for the lovely cane rod, a price I certainly couldn't match, and the lovely flyrod was gone. Can you imagine how I felt? Not like a used-car salesman after a deal, that's for sure.

I whined myself to sleep for the next several weeks. "Oh, why didn't I take that rod? It would have been perfect for my fishing," I told my wife.

I was beginning to recover from the loss of the lovely cane rod when yet another rod entered my life. This rod, another seven-and-a-half footer with two tip sections, was in need of a refinishing job: new guides, new varnish. But its reel seat was in good shape, and there was a faint tracing of labeling on the rod, though I could not quite make out the brand name. Yet, I knew a rod dealer could tell me about its genealogy and could refurbish the rod so that I could fish with it. Again, it was one of my students who wanted me to have it. He was going to join the Army, and he offered the rod to me for free!

Why is this happening to me? I wondered. How long is this going to continue? Surely, I'm not going to be tempted 40 times. This is beginning to take on some kind of religious significance!

And then I said aloud, "I can't take your rod. It's probably been in your family for years. Besides being a family heirloom, it is probably worth a lot of money. You don't want to give it away."

Fast-moving water is good habitat for brook trout. (Photo courtesy Paul Tofte)

I wrote down the addresses of the two dealers — I had them memorized by this time — and gave them to him. "Here, these people can give you a fair price for your rod if you really want to part with it," I said bravely, though I was truly covetous. I still have nightmares about turning down this remarkable offer.

Am I crazy? Should I have taken the rods? What would you have done? Could you have knowingly cheated a neighbor or a fine young man? I just couldn't do that.

However, when a former student recently walked into my classroom after school brandishing a three-piece, eight-and-a-half-foot, two-tip bamboo rod and asked me if I wanted it, I asked, "How much?"

"I'll trade it to you for your old Scout. I know you got a new truck and some of my friends told me you kept the Scout. True?"

"Yeah, I still have it, but it's not much good."

"I don't care. I can fix it up and use it for a hunting truck. What do you say? I'd like to have the Scout, and I know the flyrod might mean something to you."

This time I couldn't help myself. To me, the Scout was worthless, but to him it had some value. The rod, having no brand name on it, was probably not worth more than a hundred dollars. The trade was likely a pretty even one, so I agreed to it. After all, I can't resist temptation all the time, can I?

Chapter 17

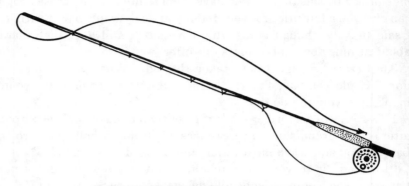

NOTES FROM MY
FLY-FISHING JOURNAL

JANUARY—FEBRUARY

Jan. 24, 1981 — This morning the local TU chapter came to look at the degraded sections of the Little Shawnee. Maybe they'll be able to get a stream improvement project going. They seemed interested anyhow. After Donna fed them and they left, I went to cut yet another load of firewood.

Feb. 19, 1973 — Today Bruce, Darrell Claar, and I went to Fisherman's Paradise. Though it was cool and overcast and the water was slightly high and cloudy, we all caught some trout. Darrell got four on streamers, Bruce got seven on grizzly midges, and I got eight on the midges, despite the water conditions. I got a real nice 13-inch brown that turned out to be the day's best fish.

Feb. 16, 1976 — This past week's lovely weather has melted most of the snow, and I had spring fever. Today Dan and I drove down to Paradise to cure our cases; we had a nice morning weather-wise, but it clouded up by noon. Dan left at 2:00. I stuck around until 3:00, when it started to rain. Dan had gotten a couple on midges. I caught six, three in the morning and three more after lunch, all on midges. From 2:00 till 3:00, I tried streamers — zip. The water was high, and there were few risers to the sparse hatch of snow flies in the cloudy run-off. But it was nice to get out, and Donna's Valentine's gift of my fishing license proved to be useful. Anyhow, the day took the "edge" off, at least for a while.

MARCH

March 11, 1972 — Today Darrell Claar and I went to Fisherman's Paradise near Bellefonte. It was the first time I've ever been there. Using Black-nosed dace streamers, he caught three trout, two browns and a rainbow. I got skunked. Maybe next time I'll be a little luckier.

March 24, 1973 — A beautiful day. Bruce and I went to Paradise this afternoon. It was mobbed! There must have been 200 people there. Even so, we both caught some trout when a midge hatch came off from 3:15 until 4:30. I got five, and Bruce got three on the size 22 grizzly midges. I missed and lost another half-dozen on this warm sunny afternoon.

March 16, 1974 — This evening, Bruce, Dan, and I went to the TU dinner at Milesburg to listen to Vincent Marinaro speak. He talked about light refraction and fly design. He noted how they influence whether a trout accepts or rejects a fly. Afterwards, I got him to autograph my copy of *A Modern Dry Fly Code*, and he invited Bruce, Dan, and me to talk with him at his camper. He and his friend, Bill Fritz, were very gracious hosts and obviously very knowledgeable fly-fisherman. They even invited us to attend the Harrisburg Flyfishers' banquet in a couple weeks. That might be neat.

March 24, 1974 — Dan and I went to Paradise today. It was sunny — but windy and cold. The creek was pretty clear, though, and we did well. Dan got 10, and I got 11 on our trusty midges. An interesting note: Vincent Marinaro said that when a trout turns completely around, he always takes the fly (if it doesn't drag). Today, at least, the trout did just that!

March 12, 1977 — Dan and I visited Paradise today. We were catching trout in the morning on our midges. But as it approached 12:00, the weather changed, and the fish quit rising. We ended up with only seven trout between us, none after noon. We talked to a commercial fly tyer there today. He said he ties 20,000 flies a year! God, it must be awful to sit hunched over a tying vise for the amount of time he must spend tying.

March 28, 1990 — 70 degrees! This afternoon I drove to a small fish-for-fun area not too far from home. The water, 46 degrees at 12:30 and 50 degrees at 3:00, had the trout stirred up. They were rising, though I didn't see any flies, even midges, on the water. So, using a size 14 Adams, I had at them, and I did really well. I landed two-dozen fine browns as I got to cover the whole project without interference! What a dandy day for March!

APRIL — SOME OPENING DAYS

April 13, 1968 — The first day of trout season. Dad, Bill (my brother), and I went fishing today. We got to the creek at 5:00 a.m. and the trout hit until about 6:30. By then they were spooky, at least the ones that hadn't been caught out. I got four trout, Dad got four, and Bill did pretty well for a nine-year-old, landing three. Dad had to leave for work at 7:00. Bill and I stayed until 10:00. It seems like more guys are on the Little Shawnee than there used to be.

April 12, 1969 — The trout opener. Using baits, I got my limit today of stocked brown trout. Dad got four, and Bill got two. It was so warm that I think I'll try flies soon.

April 14, 1973 — I'm sticking to my guns: flies only this year. Anyhow, on the Shawnee this morning at Blackwell's Meadow, I got one 13-inch trout on a Black-nosed Dace streamer. The worm and minnow fisherman were doing really well, but I wasn't even tempted. After a hoagie for lunch, I hiked to a little mountain brook I heard about last winter, and I caught 12 five- to eight-inch brook trout there on Royal Coachman wet flies. They were lovely, though tiny. It was a lovely, sunny opening day.

April 16, 1977 — I hiked in to the brook trout hollow today. It was sunny and warm, 70 degrees by noon! I got 11 gorgeous brook trout, including a double in one pool. I also missed a dozen or so! This afternoon I got three hatchery dummies on the Shawnee. They were actually rising! I'm sure tonight's scheduled monsoons will put an end to that for a while. On a bad note: I found two dead deer today along the mountain brook. The winter must've been even worse than we thought.

April 18, 1987 — As is my usual wont, I went to the walk-in brook trout stream to usher in the trout season. This year, though, I didn't fish. Instead, I had a partner who fished. Bobby, my seven-year-old son, did, and he caught and released a half-dozen brookies when he could manage to quit throwing stones! His best fish were typical eight-inchers. We didn't see any wildlife — seven-year-olds are just too noisy for that, I discovered today. He never complained about the walk, and he hooked all the trout on his own, using flies, I might add. As he grows up, I hope he continues to enjoy the outdoors, especially the fishing.

APRIL — OTHER THAN OPENING DAYS

April 18, 1969 — This evening I caught my first trout on one of my own flies. It was a little native brown trout. I missed two others that were rising. At dark, it began to rain.

Fish aren't the only wildlife found in the water. A duck watches as an angler attempts to land a brown trout.

April 21, 22, 1970 — Rich Bobb and I took a couple days off from classes to go fishing near his hunting camp. Hunting camp — it was a mansion! Day one of fishing I caught two-dozen trout and kept five for supper. He kept six. He's a good cook; the trout were delicious. On Wednesday, the 22nd, I got five more trout, and Rich got his limit. We gave them to his mom before we headed back to college after two great days "off."

April 23, 1972 — The family went to our Renovo hunting camp last night. Today, Bruce and I walked three miles in the rain to fish for brook trout. Using flies and worms, I got 30 (kept three), and Bruce did even better. When the sun came out about 11:00, the fishing in the little mountain brook became even more pleasant.

April 22, 1973 — I spent nine hours pounding creeks today, and I caught three trout for my efforts. From 5:30 until 11:00 a.m., I tried Blackwell's Meadow. Using Muddler Minnows, I got two 10-inch trout and missed several others. From 1:00 until 3:30, Bruce and I were back there, hoping for an early season hatch. However, I'm starting to believe that the hatches don't start on the Shawnee as soon as other places. We didn't see even one fly. From 5:00 to 6:00, we looked at the small branch of the Shawnee, and I got one stocked brown there on an Adams. One trout for every three hours of fishing: That's not very good.

April 27, 1974 — Sunny and 70 degrees. Bruce and I drove to north-central Pennsylvania to fish one of its well-known freestone trout streams, hoping for a hatch of flies. We lucked out. From 1:00 until 5:00 there were a few flies hatching constantly — Blue Quills and Quill Gordons. It got the fish going. I caught and released 33 trout, the most I've ever caught other than brook trout fishing. Most of the trout ran between nine and 11 inches. Three (two browns, one rainbow) in the 12-inch category were my best fish. I covered a lot of water, probably close to two miles. I fished thoroughly, covering glides, riffles, and pools the whole distance. Bruce, meanwhile, stayed in one pool, experimenting to see how body colors affected the fish. He got 12, and he thought fly size was more important than color. I got 27 of my fish on a size 14 Adams, and six on size 18 Blue Quills when I saw trout taking smaller flies. What a day! I'm glad Bruce talked me into going.

April 21, 1976 — After work, I went to the Little Juniata to try for trout. At 6:30, a fair caddis hatch came off, and I got six of the 10 trout I got up. As the hatch petered out after 7:00, a gobbler raised bloody cain across the river from me. The 90-degree weather seems to have things starting up. Maybe there will even be some early fishing at home on the Shawnee.

April 27, 1978 — What a lousy spring. It has been so cold, I can't even dream up a hatch. I drove around the Little Juniata and the Shawnee this evening, but I never got the rod out. I hope the weather warms up sometime.

April 21, 1980 — I had a wonderful day today. On a tip from my friend Walt Rosser, the Waterways Conservation Officer, I took a small trip to fish a freestone creek he told me about. "It will have Blue Quills on," Walt assured me, and it did. From 1:00 until 4:00, using a size 16 Blue Quill, I caught and released 30 small brook, brown and rainbow trout. The browns and rainbows all looked like stocked trout; the brookies appeared to be wild trout. The hatch, though never heavy, was wonderful and provided good fishing, especially after having been skunked the last two times I tried to fish. That Walt's creek is less than an hour from home is an attraction. I ought to be able to catch trout there yearly — before the Shawnee ever heats up. It's nice to have a warden for a friend.

April 17, 1985 — After work today, I fished a small, recently designated wild trout stream. It's a beauty! In a little more than an hour, I landed 10 gorgeous trout on an Adams. Eight were seven to eight-inch brook trout. The other two were chunky 10-inch browns. I hit the tail end of what appeared to be a modest hatch of Quill Gordons and Blue Quills mixed. There were two different sizes of grayish mayflies, at any rate, and the fish were working on them.

April 25, 1988 —Since we celebrated Donna's birthday yesterday, I got to fish after work today. I tried the wild trout water, and in two hours I landed 22 lovely brook and brown trout, all on a Grizzly Parachute. The best fish were several 10-inch brown trout.

On the way home, I stopped along the Little Juniata, and trout were rising to a sparse hatch of caddisflies. I hustled back into my gear and caught the nicest batch of river fish I've seen in years. I landed five between 10 and 14 inches, one 16 inches, and a dandy 18-inch brown that gave my little mountain rod a real workout. It was certainly a great afternoon, though I think it's sad that there are few times anymore that you can get an evening of fishing like this on the Little Juniata. I was just lucky, and I know it. The next guy who fishes through that stretch will probably kill every trout he catches, and it seems that there's nothing that can be done about it.

MAY

May 2, 1969 — Tonight Bruce and I sneaked into the private fishing club and fished from midnight until about 1:30. Using worms, we each got three trout. Feeling a little guilty, I threw mine back, though I wouldn't have thrown back the last one I hooked if I'd gotten

An angler's trophy is a trout, as the author's brother-in-law illustrates here.

him. I had him on about 10 minutes before I lost him. It was kind of fun to be a poacher tonight.

May 10, 1970 — It rained, but I fly-fished Blackwell's Meadow again. I took my girlfriend along. I caught only one 10-inch trout, but I put it back when she said it was too pretty to kill. She was right. I lost another fish, one of 12 or 14 inches, when I tried to lift it over a bank instead of netting it. I wasn't too happy about that. There were lots of Beaverkills on the creek this evening, but those were the only two trout I saw taking them.

May 10, 1972 — I went out to Blackwell's this evening. Light Hendrickson duns came off sparsely for a little while, and I got four eight- to 11-inch trout while they lasted. There were a few spinners (what we used to call Female Beaverkills) toward dark, but they didn't get any trout moving. The duns are tan, and some have bluish wings, while others have tan wings. They look like Light Hendricksons from what I can compare them to in my books about mayfly hatches. If they're not, they're what Vincent Marinaro called Sulphurs in *A Modern Dry Fly Code.*

May 14, 1975 — Bruce, Alex Vezza, Gary Probst, Henry Malone, and I went on an expedition today to north-central Pennsylvania. But the creeks were almost all muddied up! Pine Creek, Kettle Creek, and even most of the little ones were all roaring. We finally found one that was fishable, and we each caught a couple trout, despite beer-bleary eyes.

After that, we headed back to central Pennsylvania where the creeks are normal. At dusk, we spread out on one of Henry's pet spots, and as a light hatch of *invarias* came off, we each caught a few trout. Henry, of course, got the most, but I got the biggest one for a change, a 17-inch rainbow that gave me a real battle. So, despite rather lackluster fishing on the normally clear north-central Pennsylvania streams, today turned out all right for me!

May 15, 1977 — Today was the first decent day, numbers-wise, I've had yet this year. Dan, Mooch Irvin, and I tried the Little Juniata this morning, but there wasn't much happening. We each got a couple small trout.

This evening, on the Little Shawnee, a good *invaria* hatch and spinner fall got the trout working. From 6:30 until nearly dark, I had pretty steady action. I caught and released 18 lovely trout, all from seven to 12 inches. There are obviously a lot of trout there this year. Maybe I can find a big one to work on if I'm lucky.

May 17, 1980 — Out to Blackwell's. It was muggy, cool, and overcast, but there were finally some flies on the Little Shawnee. I got four trout from 5:00 to 6:00, all the longer flies lasted. I talked to the new weird guy. There was a Wyatt Burp type, too; I hope he doesn't come around too often. It was guys like him who cleaned out Blackwell's Meadow in the mid-1970s.

May 23, 1981 — In my effort to be a good "dad," I took Donna and Bobby on a drive for ice cream cones tonight. But, I had craftily stashed my gear in the car trunk, and on the way home, I squeezed in a half-hour of fishing to a decent hatch/spinner fall of *invarias*. Despite the cloudy water on the Little Shawnee, I managed to catch a half-dozen stocked brown trout up to 13 inches.

May 21, 1983 — A cold, drizzly day. I snuck out to the Shawnee from 3:00 to 5:00, and I hit a nice dun hatch of Sulphurs (*invarias*). Though the hatch was good, fish didn't rise well, and I could catch only 15 trout. After supper, I went back out. There were few spinners; I picked up only three small trout before calling it an evening.

May 27, 1984 — Another successful outing. After our Memorial Day meal, Bruce and I went off to his river to fish. We hit a light hatch and spinner fall of Sulphurs after 8:15. Still, he got eight nice browns. I had a good evening with five trout. One of them was 18 inches, and another was 19 inches! I really had to horse the 19-incher. Thunder and lightning were coming over a hill across the river from me, and I had to back out fast, with the fish on, to get out of the water. I just dragged him along, not worrying about whether or not I was going to lose him. I didn't.

May 13, 1985 — Blackwell's: 18 lovely wild browns. Boy, I'm glad they quit stocking the Little Shawnee, at least this section of it, with hatchery dumbbells. These wild trout are just gorgeous.

I endured a negative incident, however. A local guy had a noted entomologist/where-to-go outdoor writer on the creek. I hope he doesn't kiss-and-tell on the Shawnee. He also said that the *invarias* and *rotundas* coming off the creek are to be called "Sulphurs." Though I've been doing that for a few years, who really cares? It irritated me enough to look at his book, to see how he described Sulphur hatches, and, he called *invarias* and *rotundas* "Pale Evening Duns" in the book! I wish I'd known that when he was trying to be impressive. I guess Nick Lyons was right about certain "experts." He was the first well-known fly-fisherman I've met that seemed to have an "attitude," as my kids at school say about people like this guy. I'm still irritated about it.

May 30, 1989 — The water on the Shawnee is still high but is clearing after more monsoons. Despite the hazy, hot, humid evening (nearly 90 degrees today), I landed 18 nine- to 13-inch trout on the small branch this evening, all on a poly-winged spinner as the spinners hit the water before the duns even started. That's certainly backwards. I'm not too hopeful about a repeat tomorrow: We're supposed to have major rainstorms yet again!

JUNE

June 1, 1969 — Fished a meadow on the small branch this evening after work. The beach had few "customers" today. Anyhow, there weren't many Beaverkills hatching this evening. I managed to catch four nine-inch trout, too small to keep. After I was done, I talked to Pike DiBartolome. He told me to try to keep at it after dark, but I have enough trouble catching them during the day. But he keeps saying they run bigger after dark; so maybe I ought to give it a shot.

June 2, 1971 — I have a week and a half off before I go back to Lock Haven for summer school and to get my degree. At least it delayed my getting drafted until after the summer. I'm not looking forward to the Army and Vietnam. I've heard too much from guys who were there. Anyhow, my girlfriend and I fished the lower meadow of the small branch this evening, but the creek was silted, and I managed only one little trout.

June 3, 1974 — The little meadow on the small branch: The Light Hendricksons were on from 8:20 until dark. I got 11 trout, the best of which was 12 inches. As the season wears on, the hatches always get later and later.

June 8, 1975 — Donna, my fiancé, went with me to the catch-and-release area of a little creek this evening, though she really doesn't enjoy fishing. From 5:00 until after 8:00, I caught 33 trout on this cool, overcast day. There were a few caddisses, some dark *Stenonema* duns, and a lot of *dorothea* duns on till about 7:30. Over the years, I've finally begun to realize that cold weather in May and June brings on the hatches earlier in the day than they normally emerge, and it makes for steadier, though less-exciting action.

June 10, 1979 — The good hatches are winding down on the Shawnee. At Blackwell's, I got only five trout as only a few *invarias* came off this evening. Maybe it is time to concentrate on morning fishing now.

June 16, 1980 — Rains have totally fouled up the Shawnee and even its little branch. So this afternoon I drove around, hoping to find a clear creek. I did: the catch-and-release area! It was sunny and cold, and from 3:00 to 6:00 a nice BWO hatch came off, and I got 34 trout from six to 12 inches while it lasted. I took a sandwich break and then went back to business. A hatch and spinner fall of *dorotheas* came off

Fly-fishing is a wonderful way to spend a sunny summer day.

from 7:00 until 8:30, and I caught 21 more, tops 13 inches. I figure I would have gotten zipped on the Shawnee; so this 55-trout day is pretty special.

June 11, 1981 — My first morning adventure of the season on the Shawnee was a success. It was sunny and cool, but it warmed up nicely toward 10:00. I fished from 8:30 to 11:00, and I landed 15 modest wild browns on a Wright Caddis. The caddis will get lots of use from now on as the season progresses.

June 5, 1983 — After a family supper at Bruce and Anne's today, he and I went out to fish. The well-known creek was mobbed, so we went to the river Bruce likes. At 8:15 Sulphurs came on, and I got eight trout in the next hour. Four were modest browns, but the last four went 16, 18, 19, and 20 inches respectively! It was great! They all took a Sulphur spinner. Bruce did well, too, catching a half-dozen fine trout. But his real success this evening was "guiding" me to the pod of lunker browns.

June 11, 1984 — The hatch/spinner fall were late this evening, not starting until 8:50. Even so, I got eight decent trout in the Shawnee woods. One was an 18-inch dandy, the best trout I've ever gotten from that stretch. He never hesitated in taking a size 14 Sulphur spinner at dark. I hope nobody kills him: He's a nice one. He is the kind we need to spawn since the fish commission quit stocking this part of the Shawnee.

June 17, 1986 — I fished a little freestone stream within an hour of home from 4:00 to 6:00 this afternoon. Despite the monsoons that have totally screwed up the Shawnee, this little gem was clear and fished pretty well. Using a Grizzly Parachute, I caught and released 16 lovely brown and brook trout, mostly browns. They were decent fish too. Most ran from seven to 11 inches, with one gorgeous wild brown being an honest 15 inches! The biggest brook trout was almost 10 inches. I'm feeling pretty smug about my success.

June 25, 1987 — I fished the lower end of the Shawnee today. This morning on a caddis, I landed 18 trout ranging from six to 12 inches. I went back this evening and picked up four nice browns on a Cream Variant that matched the few flies that were on. That was once a good hatch on the Shawnee, but it's really petered out lately. After dark, I tied on a black Wooly Bugger, and it accounted for the three biggest trout of the day: 14, 16, and 17 inches. I should have fished longer, but I hadn't told Donna I might fish after dark. Even so, a 25-trout day on the Shawnee is nothing to sneeze at.

June 28, 1988 — Went up to the "Chubville" section of the Shawnee this evening, to the pool where I lost the big trout last week. Unlike the lower water, there are still some white mayflies up there. Anyhow, I did well: 10 trout! I got five on white flies and five more on the Governor after dark. Except for the last one, they were modest. The last one was a sleek 19-inch brown that sure fought well. But I don't think he is the one I lost last week: It felt much heavier than this one did. Still, I'm not complaining. I don't get too many this size in a year.

JULY

July 2, 1968 — I went out to a wooded section of the small branch of the Little Shawnee Creek this evening. I caught two small native brown trout, both about eight inches long. I used a large Dark Cahill to catch them. I also missed two trout this evening, a hot, muggy one.

July 3, 1969 — This evening I tried a yellow-bodied Adams on the Little Shawnee. I got three trout on it. Later, at midnight, I went back out with live crickets. In two hours, I got one trout, a 12-inch brown, on the crickets. I missed one or two strikes.

Unfortunately, most of my crickets have escaped and are all over our house. It's pretty noisy around the house at night from their chirping.

July 4, 1972 — Bruce and I tried the small branch this evening for the first time since the June 22 flood. The water is still really high, but in some flat pools, we each picked up two trout. There were a few flies on to get the trout going, too.

Summer on the Little Juniata River means fly-fishing for trout.

July 5, 1976 — I went out to the little branch this morning at 7:00 (it rained until then after late-night thunderstorms). I used a size 10 Blacknosed Dace for almost three hours, and I had 14 hits as the rain started back up. Of those hits, I landed five trout, the largest being a dandy 14-inch wild brown. I would like to hook a better percentage of the fish that hit my streamers. It is always like today: I get about one out of about every three trout that hit my streamers. When I got home, Donna assured me that I was crazy to fish on a day like this. But I know better: The trout were worth it.

July 12, 1980 — This morning I was on a foggy Little Juniata River by 6:30. I fished with a Stonefly and a little black nymph for three hours. I got only five trout, the best a chunky 13-inch brown. By the time I walked back to my Scout, it must've been 85 degrees. It is going to be another scorcher.

July 14, 1982 — This morning I visited a little limestone run, looking for Tricos. No luck. I did manage 10 trout from seven to 12 inches, all on a Wright Caddis fished to the water. This evening, after a trip for ice cream, I went night fishing for a couple of hours. I got two trout on a Leadwing Coachman. One was a 12-inch rainbow; the other was a dandy 17-inch brownie that carried on wildly in the dark. I was fishing only 50 yards from an arc light, and the light didn't seem to bother the trout at all. (It makes it less spooky, too!)

July 22, 1983 — It was a stale, humid morning, and the Shawnee was a little off-color from the rains. I decided to try wet flies along the stretch that bends away from the roads. I got only two trout, a nine-inch beauty and the biggest trout I've ever caught. He was an ugly old brown of nearly 21 inches. He took a size 10 Black Ant. After I hooked him, he did a lot of bulldogging along the bottom before I could work him into the shallows and beach him, measure him, and then release him. Afterwards, I fished for another hour-and-a-half, trying both wet flies and a Wright Caddis, but I didn't move another fish. Even so, after landing the bruiser, I didn't really care.

July 16, 1986 — I drove to the little limestoner for Tricos today, and before an 8:30 monsoon washed it out completely, I had landed a dozen eight- to 12-inch brown trout. They were really easy. Every one took a size 18 Trico spinner willingly. You don't always have to use those itty-bitties that the experts tell you to use.

July 27, 1987 — I found trout taking Tricos on the small branch of the Shawnee today in a place I've never seen the trout take a Trico before. Usually they just ignore them. Not today, though. Anyhow, before I quit at 11:00, I had 10 trout, eight on Tricos, two on a caddis. They ran nice, too. Most were nine to 11 inches, and one, at the old railroad bridge, was the nicest 14-inch wild brown I've ever seen — bright red spots, butter-yellow belly, and fat. Maybe I'm wrong, but I think the trout have gotten a lot prettier on the Shawnee since they quit stocking it with hatchery trout.

July 30, 1988 — I felt like trying new water today; so I drove to one of the state's fly-fishing-only projects. In a little more than two hours, I covered its mile of water. Using a Wright Caddis, I landed a dozen 10- to 12-inch trout, all browns but one. It was a fat rainbow. They all appeared to be stocked trout. They must get a lot of pressure, too. I had a dozen or more short rises, typical of trout that have been caught and released a lot. It was kind of neat to look for new water: I don't do that much anymore.

July 31, 1989 — A 50-trout day. In less than four hours this afternoon on a little freestone stream about two hours from home, I covered about two miles of water, using a caddis. The trout were on the prowl and rose hard all afternoon. I caught a nice mixture of brooks and browns as the trout rose eagerly all afternoon. They were everywhere: pools, riffles, eddies. I should have landed twice as many as I did: Even after 20 years of fly-fishing, I pull too darned hard when trout rise splashily. It was a wonderful excursion. The creek was in super shape, unlike my home creeks, which are still fouled up from this summer's constant rains. This was only the fourth day I've fished this month, and all four days have been away from my home creeks.

AUGUST

Aug. 4, 1971 — I was home last night for a job interview. I'm pretty sure they're going to hire me, even though I told them I was probably going to be drafted. Anyhow, this evening I fished at Blackwell's Meadow, and I caught three nice trout. The weird guy was there, too. I talked to him briefly. He'd caught four on wet flies. I kept my largest trout this evening for a meal of trout and potatoes. The rest of the family is on vacation at the shore.

Aug. 8, 1974 — Dan and I fished a little limestone creek with Tricos this morning. The trout were tough, but I got five, and he got three. All were small, though we both lost decent trout of 12 inches or so.

This evening I went out to the small branch of the Little Shawnee. Using a Yellow Adams, I caught three of the nine trout I got up. I left early to come home to listen to President Nixon's resignation speech. Even though he really screwed up over Watergate, he suspended the draft before the Army could get me, and I feel badly for him.

Aug. 6, 1976 — My best morning for a while. I got to the Little Shawnee at about 7:15 and fished until 11:00. It was a lovely morning: sunny and clear and no haze. The fishing was okay, too. Using the Stonefly and little black nymph, I landed 10 trout and lost a couple others. Most ran eight to 10 inches, though I got several in the 12-inch range. As I walked back to my Scout, I saw a couple bait fishermen. I'm sure they weren't releasing any of the trout they caught.

Aug. 8, 1977 — Dan and I drove to Newville today and fished Big Spring Creek — right where it comes out of a hatchery. There were a lot of guys there. From 8:30 to noon, we fished over steadily rising trout, and I caught 16 of them on a grizzly midge, mostly in one pool. One was a 15-inch brook trout; another was an ugly 16-inch brown. I spent an hour working on a huge brown that was lying under a log. He ignored all the wets, nymphs, and streamers I showed him, and I finally conceded defeat. Dan also got several nice trout. The fishing there was crowded, a lot like Paradise. Even so, it's worth traveling like this on occasion.

Aug. 12, 1981 — Fished the wooded section of the Shawnee today. Going down to the last flat, I used wets and got five, all on a Leadwing Coachman. I put on a caddis to fish back upstream, and I got five more. All the fish ran eight to 12 inches — but one. He was a heavy 19-inch brown that I thought was going to break me in a tangle of roots. But he didn't, and I succeeded in beaching him after a spirited tussle. After taping him, I revived him and let him go. It's amazing that a trout like that could make it on the Shawnee with all the pressure it gets from meat fishermen. I think this trout is almost as big as the one I'm after on upstream at the walnut tree.

Aug. 17, 1983 — Spent the morning at Blackwell's, and I caught eight trout. I got only one going down on wets, under the roots of a big willow tree that is sure to wash out the next time there's high water. He was a heavy 19-inch brown, and he took a size 10 Black Ant. Coming back upstream using a caddis, I got seven more, all seven to 10 inches. Sadly, I can see the banks of the pasture steadily eroding away. I wish I could do something about it.

Aug. 18, 1985 — Dan drove his new car to limestone country today. First stop: Falling Spring. The Tricos were good from 9:00-11:00, and we each got a half dozen nice trout, all 10 inches or better. Dan got a 17-inch brown; I got an 18-inch rainbow that I even got a picture of. Usually having my camera with me jinxes me with decent trout.

After that, we drove to Big Spring, but it looked awful; so we went to the Letort and pounded it under the 90-degree afternoon sun. I got one 12-inch brown trout for all the effort. We're getting too old to slog through the Letort swamps in 90-degree weather.

On the way home, we fished another little creek, and we each landed three more trout before hordes of mosquitoes chased us off. Though we were both pooped, we agreed that limestone country fishing is a nice alternative to the fishing at home — sometimes.

Aug. 24, 1986 — Today was the last day before school starts, and I have to go back to work. I spent the morning in the upper meadow of the little branch, and between 9:30 and noon I got six trout, three on the caddis, three on Tricos. The fish were all nine to 10 inches but one. He was the trout of the summer, a heavy brown of over 19 inches that, amazingly, took a Trico! I actually thought the fish was a log until he rose: Fish just don't grow that big on the little branch. Anyhow, he rose for my first cast, and I missed him. I thought I'd blown it, but he kept rising; so I tried him again. He took my size 22 Trico again, and I hooked him this time. He didn't fight very well: It was a battle against dead weight as I kept him from going under a barbed wire fence. He is the largest trout I've ever gotten on a Trico — and on the small branch. A nice way to end my summer vacation.

Aug. 21, 1989 — Bobby's 10th birthday. He is growing up awfully fast. Since we celebrated yesterday, I was free to pester the trout. This morning, I fished along the road on the lower Shawnee, but I managed only one 10-inch trout, my worst day for a while.

I saved my fishing day this evening. Bobby and Donna were swimming in the new pool so I was on my own. I drove up to the middle Shawnee to pool fish until dark. There were a few risers, and using White Bombers, I landed four trout. Three were in the 10- to 12-inch category. The last one was my best trout of the summer, a nice 19-inch brown that battled mightily into the darkness. After I unhooked him, it took me several minutes to revive him so he could swim off — by the light of my flashlight!

The fly-fishing "bug" can bite anyone — young or old — at any time.

SEPTEMBER

Sept. 7, 1970 — My last trip to the little branch of the Shawnee before I head back to Lock Haven for my final year of college. I got three nine- to 10-inch trout on a Yellow Adams this evening, and I released them all. I haven't killed a trout since July 8. They really are too pretty to kill indiscriminately. While on the creek, I saw a pure white animal. It wasn't a muskrat. It was either a mink or an early whitened weasel. It was shocking.

Sept. 1, 2, 1973 — Bruce, Dan, Alex Vezza and I fished limestone country for two days. We spent mornings and afternoons on the Letort, and we spent our first evening on the Yellow Breeches. It was muddied by heavy rains the second day. We all caught trout: Alex, 12; me, 11; Bruce, 10; Dan, 5. But it was tough fishing. The hatch of White Millers on the Yellow Breeches is unreal, and catching trout with so many flies and so many fishermen around is difficult.

The high point of the excursion was an invitation to attend the fly-fishermen's bash along the Letort. Well-known angler, Ed Shenk, told us to come. We saw the famous Vincent Marinaro, and we listened to Letort legend Charles Fox tell tales until past midnight.

He is a real gentleman. It was a nice experience to be around so many well-known fly-fishermen at one time.

Sept. 10, 1975 — After my cross country team's practice, John Naugle, one of my former runners, and I tried a section of a local creek. John tried streamers without luck. I could manage only four small fries on caddisses. On such a nice day, I thought we'd do better.

Sept. 18, 1977 — I finally got in some fishing today. In 45 minutes after work, I caught five small trout on the small branch on a caddis. Tonight, I sent in my letter of resignation to the private fishing club I was in for a couple of years. Though it is a nice place and there are some nice guys in it, there was some backbiting and bickering going on that I didn't want to be part of. Plus, I only fished there nine or 10 times in two years. It seemed like legal poaching. I didn't enjoy being a member of a private club very much. I really think that streams should be open to public fishing with some special regulations. Anyhow, I've gotten out of what I felt was a bad situation.

Sept. 16, 1980 — A beautiful autumn day, and I fished hard. From 12:00 to 3:00, I caught 16 modest trout at Blackwell's. They wouldn't take my caddis, but after I put on an Adams, the fishing really heated up. This evening, from 5:00 to 7:00, I got five more on the Adams on the lower end. They were all modest fish except one, a nice 14-inch wild brown. I'm sort of "fished out" right now.

Sept. 4, 1982 — My mother died today from her third stroke. She was really a special woman. As people said, she really meant it when she asked, "How are you?" She mothered me effectively: helping me through personal crises; helping me avoid joining a fraternity I wanted to stay out of; craftily getting our family doctor to tell me that I needed to quit drinking beer the summer I turned 21. One of my favorite memories is the night that she and Donna were going to look for me in the county's barrooms when Donna thought I was mad at her and I was fishing. I'm lucky to have had two women — Donna and Mom — who have loved me so much. I'm going to miss my mother. As Dad says, she was the glue in our family.

Sept. 22, 1984 — A super afternoon. From 1:30 to 4:00 I fished the wooded section of the Little Shawnee. There was a hatch of little grayish mayflies *(Baetis?)* on. A size 18 Blue Quill would've been a good size match, but I didn't have any with me; so I used a size 16 Adams. It was close enough: The trout gullibly sucked it in all afternoon, and I ended up catching 21 wild brown trout up to 13 inches. The weather sunny, 75 degrees — a wonderful first day of autumn. It also reinforces my belief that you don't usually have to match a hatch exactly: You just have to be close.

Sept. 15, 1988 — Following after-school basketball (I'm trying to play again, at age 38, after not playing much since college), I had enough energy to sneak out to Blackwell's for an hour. It was amazing. I got 13 trout, including two rainbows! Where did they come from? They must have drifted down from the stocked water during the drought. My last trout was special. I'd seen him last week, busting through the foam along a downed tree, had hooked him on an Adams but lost him. This evening, at dusk, I floated the White Bomber along the foam, and he sucked it in. He didn't tangle me this evening as he did last week, and about seven or eight minutes after I'd hooked him, I got him on the gravel on my side of the creek. He was about 20 inches long, heavy — a really nice brown. I hope he does a good job of fertilizing eggs next month!

Sept. 11, 1989 — The last day of my dream fishing trip to Wyoming-Montana. After a frigid morning, the fishing picked up on the Bighorn. About noon, I ran into fish taking Sulphurs (Westerners call them Pale Morning Duns), and for the next two-and-a-half hours I was busy. I landed 10 of the trout I hooked, all over 15 inches. The largest was a 20-inch brown, though he wasn't as heavy as a couple an inch or two smaller. I hated to leave at 2:30, but I had a five-hour drive to Bozeman to get a room and to get ready to fly home tomorrow. (I could've fished another hour: the drive took only four hours.)

It was an enjoyable trip, despite having cold, rainy weather for four of my seven fishing days. Around Yellowstone Park the first three days, I caught a lot of fish, including some nice cutthroats to a BWO hatch during a cold rain. This was at Buffalo Ford on the Yellowstone. I was glad that some folks from Wisconsin urged me to go to the Bighorn. Though the scenery there wasn't much and I was lucky to get a room without any reservations, the size of the trout there was amazing. In three half-days of fishing and one full day, I didn't catch a trout under 15 inches! That just blows my mind. It also lets me realize how good our Little Juniata River could be with slot limits like those on the Bighorn. The 22-inch rainbow that was my first Bighorn trout was one of the heaviest I've ever caught, too.

It was interesting to listen to other guys talk in the restaurant after a day's fishing on the Bighorn. They've got lots of money and fish all over the place. Watching them on the stream was also interesting. They have beautiful gear and look like neoprene clones of each other. And they obviously like to fly-fish.

Any regrets about the trip? Sure. I wish I'd had $200 more than I did to hire a guide for a day on the Bighorn. The guys in the drift

The author's youngest partner — his son, Bobby, shown here with a small brook trout.

boats were using nymphs with bobbers — they were really bobbers, not strike indicators — and were catching at least three or four trout for every one that I caught. Though I don't know if that's really fly-fishing, I would have tried it to get 40 to 50 trout a day of the size I was catching. I also regret that the weather wasn't a little better: I could have nearly doubled my fishing time. I also missed my family more than I thought I would!

Even so, it was a real nice experience for me to get to the West, joining the 20th century by finally flying in an airplane and getting to fish rivers I've heard so much about. I hope to go back someday.

OCTOBER/NOVEMBER

Oct. 7, 1973 — After attending yesterday's TU seminar at Penn State, Dan, Bruce, and I fished at Paradise today. It was cold, cloudy, and windy. Even so, we all got a few fish. Dan got five, I got three, and Bruce landed two. My 17-inch rainbow was the biggest one we caught.

Oct. 15, 1977 — After a morning of squirrel hunting (really, scouting for wild turkeys), I fished Blackwell's in the afternoon sun. I managed 11 modest trout on the Adams. A 12-inch brown was tops. I expected to see some spawning redds, but I didn't find one all afternoon.

Oct. 16, 1980 — Fished the water of the middle Shawnee today, and I was rewarded with nine trout. There were trout taking caddisses, and three of the ones I got were actually rising on their own. One was a 16-inch holdover brown. There were lot of trout in the shallows; they must be getting ready to spawn.

Oct. 12, 1985 — On an Adams, I caught 15 trout ranging from nine to 14 inches this afternoon. They're really active in the low, clear water, and are obviously feeding up before spawning. I saw one redd above the bridge at Blackwell's. Besides the 15, I also caught a half-dozen little guys practicing to be trout and one other: an 18-inch brown. Boy, was she gorgeous in her autumn colors! It was a nice change from the firewood cutting I've been doing.

Oct. 15, 1987 — I am not at all disappointed with today! It was a gorgeous autumn afternoon, and the trout were really out feeding. In the wooded section of the Little Shawnee, I caught and released 14 beautiful wild brown trout, all nine inches or better. About half were rising on their own, and size 18 BWOs worked on them. The others took the old, reliable Adams. No redds: Spawning seems to occur later than it used to on the Shawnee. The trout used to be actively spawning by about now. I haven't seen one redd yet this fall.

Nov. 7, 1989 — Today is the first time I've ever given November trout fishing a try; I'm usually working and hunting after work, but

I'm on a sabbatical. I went to the little branch for the afternoon, and I landed a half-dozen small trout. But there were hundreds of trout out spawning. There were redds all over the place! I saw nice trout, too. Several looked to be in the 16- to 18-inch range! I saw three dead ones, too (spawn stress?), one of about 18 inches, two about a foot long each. The trout were pretty aggressive, chasing each other, and I probably could've gotten a few more with streamers or nymphs. But I guess it's really time to let them alone for a while, at least until next spring anyhow.

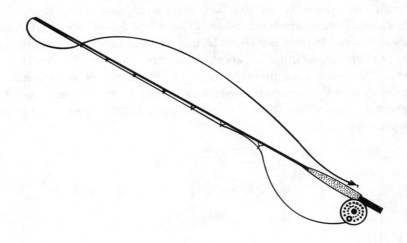

Favorite Dry Flies

ADAMS

Hook — size 14, 16 dry fly hook
Tail — grizzly feather fibers
Body — gray muskrat fur
Wings — grizzly hackle points
Hackle — one brown, one grizzly, mixed

GRIZZLY PARACHUTE

Hook — size 14, 16 dry fly hook
Tail — grizzly feather fibers
Body — gray muskrat fur
Wing — white calf tail
Hackle — grizzly, wound parachute style

SULPHUR SPINNER

Hook — size 14, 16 dry fly hook
Tail — ginger feather fibers
Body — tan spun fur
Wing — white poly yarn, laid perpindicular to hook shank
Hackle — none

WHITE BOMBER

Hook — size 12 dry fly hook
Tail — cream feather fibers
Body — cream spun fur
Wings — white calf tail, not split
Hackle — white/cream hackle feather, wound parachute style

WRIGHT CADDIS

Hook — size 14, 16 dry fly hook
Body — peacock herl, ribbed with gold tinsel
Wing — tan feather fibers, laid back over body
Hackle — tan or ginger

SULPHUR COMPARADUN

Hook — size 14, 16 dry fly hook
Tail — ginger feather fibers, split
Body — tan spun fur
Wing — tan deer hair from a deer mask
Hackle — none

TRICO SPINNER

Hook — size 18, 22 dry fly hook
Tail — 2 or 3 dun feather fibers
Body — black spun fur, wound lightly
Wing — white poly yarn, laid perpindicularly to hook
Hackle — none

CROWE BEETLE

Hook — size 14, 16 dry fly hook
Body — none, or green peacock herl
Wing case — black deer dair, tied in at bend of hook, then pulled to
            the eye of the hook and tied down

Favorite Underwater Flies

BLACK ANT

Hook — size 10, 12 wet fly hook
Body — two humps, built up of tying thread and lacquered
Hackle — one black hackle, between the humps

SULPHUR EMERGER

Hook — size 14 *dry* fly hook
Body — tan spun fur
Tail — ginger feather fibers
Hackle — ginger, clipped on top
Wing case — tan nylon from a woman's stocking, extending only a third of the way to the bend

LEADWING COACHMAN

Hook — size 10, 12 wet fly hook
Body — peacock herl
Wing — gray duck quill, laid back over body
Hackle — one brown hackle feather

WOOLY BUGGER — BLACK

Hook — size 6 or 8 wet fly hook, 3XL
Tail — thick clump of black marabou feathers
Body — black spun fur or black chenille
Hackle — grizzly, palmered the entire length of the hook

* Note: I prefer not to weight this fly as other anglers do.

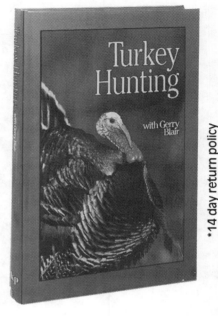